A world of prayer : spiritual leaders, activists, and humanitarians share their favorite prayers

A WORLD OF PRAYER

A WORLD OF PRAYER

Spiritual Leaders, Activists and Humanitarians Share their Favorite Prayers

Edited by Rosalind Bradley

Maryknoll, New York 10545

Founded in 1970, Orbis Books endeavors to publish works that enlighten the mind, nourish the spirit, and challenge the conscience. The publishing arm of the Maryknoll Fathers and Brothers, Orbis seeks to explore the global dimensions of the Christian faith and mission, to invite dialogue with diverse cultures and religious traditions, and to serve the cause of reconciliation and peace. The books published reflect the views of their authors and do not represent the official position of the Maryknoll Society. To learn more about Maryknoll and Orbis Books, please visit our website at www.maryknollsociety.org.

Published by Orbis Books, P.O. Box 302, Maryknoll, NY 10545-0302.

Manufactured in the United States of America

Library of Congress Cataloging-in-Publication Data

A world of prayer : spiritual leaders, activists, and humanitarians share their favorite prayers / edited by Rosalind Bradley.
p. cm.
Includes bibliographical references.
ISBN 978-1-57075-952-9 (cloth)
Prayers. I. Bradley, Rosalind.
BL560.W655 2012
204'.33—dc23

2011039721

In gratitude to my twin brother Martin Manser
and to my
Companions in Dialogue
(Imam Afroz Ali, Julian Droogan, Charlie Hogg,
Greg Johns, David Mills and Fr. Herman Roborgh, SJ)

Your Light is in all forms,
Your Love in all beings.
Allow us to recognize You
in all Your holy names and forms.

—Hazrat Inayat Khan (1882–1927)
(first Great Sufi Master who taught in the West)

CONTENTS

ACKNOWLEDGMENTS

I would like to first thank all the contributors to this book. Their inspiring insights enabled me to capture a glimpse into contemporary prayers and reflections from around the world.

I am also very grateful to the following people who helped me prepare this manuscript: Martin Manser, Sally Charkos, Fr. Herman Roborgh, SJ, Trevor Dalziell, Peter Kirkwood, Tom Stillwell, Dr. Julie Crawford, Jill Taylor, Ania Marzec-Manser, Diana Baird, Aviva Dautch, Tim Barnes, Paul Maloney, and librarian Deborah Malcolm for sourcing many books to verify texts.

The following individuals also assisted in suggesting and securing some of the contributors: Nobuko Aizawa, Pilar Ballesteros, Gill Burrows, Yvonne Chandler, Ven. Thubten Chokyi, Ben Churcher, Sr. Susan Connelly, RSJ, Rasheeda Cooper, Liz Budd Ellmann, Robert Ellsberg, Tim Fischer, Fr. Laurence Freeman, Sherry Gregory, Lesley and Jim Hamilton, Nathalie Hayes, Helen Hill, Phillip Hinton, Majid Hussein, Judith Ish-Horowicz, Miriam Ish-Horowicz, Kathryn James, Anne Kearney, Rev'd Dr. Hugh Kempster, Peta Keaney, Zuleyha Keskin, Leona Kieran, Fr. Ross Jones, SJ, Caroline and Neil Lawrence, Sr. Trish Madigan, OP, Benny Manser, Alison Mathie, Liz McCarthy, Cathy McGowan, Jane Mills, Rabbi Rachel Montagu, Genevieve Nelson, Gail O'Brien, Canon Dr. Paul Oestreicher, Mehmet Ozalp, Teresa Pirola, Agnieszka Piszcz, Pauline Peters, Canon Patience Purchas, Patricia Roberts, Prue Robertson,

Frances Rush, Elena Arreguy Sala, Fazila Sarod, Karen Shipp, Rula Shubeita, Kulwinder Singh, Rev. Austin Smith, Johanna Sierraalta, Rev. Helen Summers, The Very Rev. David Thomas, Peter Thomson, Jenna Tregarthen, Nikki Tregarthen, Ruth Wylie, and Cheery Zahau.

My Companions in Dialogue—Imam Afroz Ali, Julian Droogan, Charlie Hogg, Greg Johns, David Mills, and Fr. Herman Roborgh, SJ —were also very encouraging as were the advisory group who included the above mentioned Peter Kirkwood and Fr. Herman Roborgh, SJ, as well as Mary McInerney and Judi Taylor.

The spirit of generosity with which so many copyright holders responded to requests was affirming, and to them I offer my deep appreciation.

Sincere thanks also to Robert Ellsberg and Doris Goodnough at Orbis Books—Robert, for his ongoing guidance and enthusiasm, and Doris for her support and attention to detail regarding the many permission queries.

And finally, to my family I offer my love and thanks for their constant encouragement while I was compiling this book: to my husband Steve, children Samuel, Jessica, and Nicholas, and my dear stepmother Norma Manser.

INTRODUCTION

Prayer is a universal human activity transcending time and cultures. It is the essence of all belief systems and a way of communicating with the divine, whom the Great Sufi Master, Hazrat Inayat Khan, describes so beautifully in his prayer *Salat*: "*Your Light is in all forms, Your Love in all beings. Allow us to recognize You in all Your holy names and forms.*"

A World of Prayer presents favorite prayers and personal contemplations chosen by spiritual leaders, activists, and humanitarians from different faiths. The book demonstrates the common values shared by different religious traditions and expresses the wisdom that can be found across a range of faiths and practices. Contributors include Bahai'is, Brahma Kumaris, Buddhists, Christians, Hindus, Jews, Muslims, Sikhs, and Taoists. The prayers offer praise and thanks and call us to deepen our inner capacity for compassion through meditation and inner peace. It is my hope that these contributions will provide fresh insight into the heart of different faiths, and that acceptance of their diversity will, in some small way, help to break down religious stereotypes.

In the process of compiling this interfaith anthology, I have come to realize that the concept of this book has been bubbling within me for years. Despite my Jewish heritage, I had a very secular upbringing, and it was not until my early twenties, while I was working as a volunteer teacher in the remote Sepik area of Papua New Guinea, that I first became aware of different religious traditions. In the area where I lived spiritual practices ranged from the traditional "haus tambarans" or spirit houses to the teachings of Catholic missionaries and those of pastors from the Assemblies of God and Seventh Day Adventist Churches. At the same time, my twin brother, back in the UK, had become passionate about his new Christian faith. Subconsciously, I think these experiences stimulated a curiosity in me about the human need for the sacred and about people's spirituality. They also encouraged my own quest for a spiritual identity, a quest that culminated in my embracing Christianity, initially in the Anglican tradition, and later in the Catholic community.

During my subsequent work for international development organizations and through volunteering, I met people whose cultural, social, ethnic, and religious backgrounds were very different from my own: people from Eritrea to El Salvador and from Bosnia to Burma. World events activated my interest in interfaith dialogue and led me to help found a Sydney-based interfaith group called "Companions in Dialogue," which meets regularly for respectful conversation and reflection.

It seems to me that religion has had a higher profile in the world since "9/11" and the London 2005 bombings, both of which deeply affected me. Our current global situation with its ongoing tensions, wars, and conflicts has convinced me of the importance of finding ways to transcend religious divides and foster greater understanding and mutual respect between the world's religions. The result of this quest is a book that highlights the diversity of world religions in a positive and constructive light. I hope that *A World of Prayer* also shows that we are all members of one human family who can share the divine nature at the deepest level of the Spirit.

I believe that each of the world's main religions offers insight into the mystery of human life, as each reflects its own cultural and historical context. I also believe that no one faith should assume superiority over another in the quest for truth. All have the right to practice and profess their own beliefs. Although the world's major religions share similar views about the ethical and moral values of life, these religions are *not* the same. Each tradition embraces its own unique practices and has distinctive nuances. In *A World of Prayer,* I hope to shed new light on these differences and encourage readers to enrich their own faith while at the same time being more open to understanding other religions.

I am often asked how I chose the contributors. I looked for participants known for their spiritual leadership or their humanitarianism. Contributors include people who speak out for the voiceless, are active in social justice, human rights, peacemaking, and environmentalism, and those working toward interreligious understanding and cooperation. Some contributors are household names; others are held in high esteem in their country or among their peers. Others are "quiet achievers." I am truly grateful to all contributors (and their colleagues) for their generous responses and for the patience and energy they displayed in their dealings with me. I wrote to over five hundred people, trying hard to maintain a balance in terms of gender and tradition. At the final count, women made up just under half of the contributors. Interestingly, in my many brainstorming sessions with friends and colleagues, men's names were almost always suggested first! I am aware that I have only "scratched the surface"; there are indeed many more inspiring women and men active in our world today. Also, this book of world prayers does not—and cannot—include all of today's evolving religious traditions.

Several important themes emerge within the prayers. These themes include the importance of meditation and inner peace, compassion, gratitude and forgiveness, the love *of* God and *for* God, the oneness of humanity, having courage, a sense of personal calling, engaging with neighbors, embracing diversity, the way to enlightenment, working for justice, our connection to nature, and faith in action.

Many contributions to *A World of Prayer* have inspired me in the daily interplay of my own work and prayer, as I endeavor to see God in all things. A stirring passage by Rumi, the thirteenth-century mystic, conveys the oneness of humanity: "*I speak of plural souls in name alone.*" Martha Postlethwaite's encouraging words to "*create a clearing in the dense forest of your life*" serves as a reminder of the importance of being centered. And the poetic Arabic phrase "*Bismillah al rahman al rahim,*" which heads all but one of the Qur'anic chapters, has given me insight into the essence of Islam.

Other contributors have chosen tender verses from the Old Testament, such as those sung during the Day of Atonement, the most sacred date in the Jewish year; inspiring words by Sr. Mary Lou Kownacki, OSB, "*. . . I bow to the God within each heart . . .*"; a Taoist meditation; a Brahma Kumaris prayer; enlightened words by the eighth-century Buddhist sage Shantideva, and John Main's affirmative, words which I recite daily during Christian meditation: "*Lead us into that mysterious silence where your love is revealed to all who call—Maranatha, Come Lord.*" Many other powerful texts—from a vast array of sources ranging from the founder of the Baha'i Faith, Baha'u'llah, to T. S. Eliot, from Hinduism's *The Holy Vedas* to the Sikh writings *Sri Guru Granth Sahib*—beckon the reader.

The sections of this book are arranged in alphabetical order of contributors. The format includes a short biographical note on each contributor followed by a favorite passage and the contributor's reflections on this choice. Further information on the source of each passage and other relevant information can be found at the end of the book.

Profits from the sale of this book will go to the UK charity St. Ethelburga's Centre for Reconciliation and Peace in the City of London. The Centre, which arose from the ruins of a medieval city church destroyed by an Irish Republican Army bomb in 1993, works to promote understanding of the relationship between faith and conflict. Programs include exploring new ways of working with mixed faith groups, encouraging youth to refuse violence, sharing personal stories between faiths, and regular performances by musicians and poets from areas of conflict. The Centre's unique Bedouin Tent offers a safe and sacred space for authentic dialogue about divisive issues. (See page 212 for more information.)

A World of Prayer is a sequel to *Mosaic*, a compilation of prayers and reflections chosen by inspiring Australians, which was published by ABC Books in 2008. *Mosaic* was a response to the London bombings of 2005 and became a catalyst for my interest in interfaith exploring with an "open heart."

In compiling this interfaith book, I have been humbled by contact with so many inspiring people who are striving to make a difference in the world, fascinated by the many rich and meaningful texts I have read, and spiritually uplifted by engaging with the diversity of prayers sent to me by contributors and by the intimacy of their shared personal reflections.

Completing this project has answered some questions but raised others. I am now content to allow my faith to ebb and flow, to live the mystery. I am truly grateful for this experience. "*Be still and know that I am God*" (Psalm 46:10) is a phrase I love for its meditative overtones and for its invitation to enter into the eternal "now" of God. I trust that many of these prayers will inspire and nourish as you read and reflect upon them.

Rosalind Bradley
August 2011
www.mosaicbook.com.au

SWAMI AGNIVESH

Swami Agnivesh is a prominent social justice activist in India. Committed to ending bonded labor and forced child labor, he founded the Bonded Labour Liberation Front in 1981, which helped free more than 175,000 people. He has also campaigned for a National Minimum Wage, for women's rights, and for Dalits (Untouchables) to enter Hindu temples. Swami Agnivesh's many books include Hinduism in the New Age *and* The Other India. *His campaigns and struggles against religious fundamentalism have led to national and international recognition, including the Rajiv Gandhi National Sadbhavana Award and the Right Livelihood Award in 2004 (www.swamiagnivesh.com).*

Where the mind is without fear and the head is
held high;
Where knowledge is free;
Where the world has not been broken up into
fragments
by narrow domestic walls;
Where words come out from the depth of truth;
Where tireless striving stretches its arms towards
perfection;
Where the clear stream of reason has not lost its
way
into the dreary desert sand of dead habit;
Where the mind is led forward by thee into
ever-widening thought and action–
Into that heaven of freedom, my Father, let my
country awake.

–Rabindranath Tagore

I have always believed that prayer is nothing but preparation for social action—the only way to connect to the divine is through the philosophy of transcendence. In this prayer, Tagore (a Nobel Laureate from India) transcends his narrow boundaries and prepares himself for ameliorative social action without any biases and with complete freedom.

CHUNGLIANG AL HUANG

Chungliang Al Huang is a philosopher, performing artist, and internationally acclaimed Tao master. He is founder-president of the Living Tao Foundation and director of the international Lan Ting Institute based in the sacred mountains in China and on the Oregon coast in the United States (www.livingtao.org). Chungliang is a research scholar of the Academia Sinica, a fellow of the World Academy of Art and Science, and author of many books, including Embrace Tiger, Return To Mountain, *and* Quantum Soup. *He is co-author with Alan Watts of* Tao: The Watercourse Way, *and with Dr. Jerry Lynch of* Thinking Body, Dancing Mind.

May I always follow the Way of Earth,
Follow the Way of Heaven,
Follow the Way of Tao, follow the Way of
Nature.
So that Heaven, Human, Earth can become
ONE Harmonious Whole.
Love and harmony pervade, and Peace on Earth
for ALL.

—Tao Te Ching

I was born in China and my earliest learning consisted of the classical "Three Pillars of Asian Wisdom"—self-cultivation through Confucian ethics, Taoist ecological balance between humans and nature, and Buddhist spiritual awareness to cultivate empathy and compassion.

Now, as a world citizen in my senior years, I have continued to abide by these three pillars, integrating the living philosophies of Confucianism, Taoism, and Buddhism to provide spiritual and philosophical guidance in everyday life. In my personal prayer, I often still think and chant in Chinese, including these lines from Tao Te Ching.

Confucian teaching helps us to find harmony with other human beings; Taoist teaching helps us to be in harmony with our own true nature and Nature itself; Buddhist teaching helps us to have empathy and compassion with all sentient beings and to sustain our spiritual essence in the eternal NOW.

JAMES ALISON

James Alison, who was born in London, is a priest, theologian, and author. After studies with the Dominicans in Mexico and in Oxford, United Kingdom, and with the Jesuits in Brazil, he has become a traveling teacher, lecturer, and retreat leader. Having worked in Bolivia, Chile, and the United States as well as his native England, he now lives in Brazil. His principal work mines the thought of René Girard as a rich source for theology. James Alison is also known for his firm but gentle persistence in promoting dialogue and understanding in the Church with regard to gay issues.

Nada te turbe,	May nothing wind you up,
nada te espante,	Nothing affright you;
todo se pasa,	Everything comes and goes
Dios no se muda,	God, still, just there;
la paciencia	Through patience
todo lo alcanza;	All will be achieved.
quien a Dios tiene	If you have God,
nada le falta:	You lack nothing:
solo Dios basta.	God alone will do.

—Teresa of Avila (trans. James Alison)

As someone who lives with a deep sense of panic just below the surface of things, the agitation of being driven by the *turba* or crowd, I find St. Teresa's pithy call back to God very comforting. She kept this brief annotation in her breviary, and I like to think of her coming across it, as something forgotten, when many other things were going on in her life, then finding herself taken to a place of fullness, of being sated. She knows who the real protagonist of all things is, how relaxing that knowledge is, and how much can be let go in its light.

I love the short, sharp, dry word-gestures with which she expresses herself—wonderfully Castilian. That style can't really be reproduced in English, so I have taken the liberty of being suggestive rather than literal in my translation.

BROTHER ALOIS, PRIOR OF TAIZÉ

Brother Alois is a German Catholic who has held French nationality since 1984. In 1974 he entered the Taizé Community, an ecumenical self-supporting Christian monastic community made up of Catholics and Protestants who live together as a living sign of reconciliation among Christians. Brother Alois has been the community's prior since 2005, succeeding the founder Brother Roger (www.taize.fr).

"Who can condemn us since Jesus is praying for us?" As I listen to young people speaking personally to me, I often wonder what can be the source of the feeling they have of being condemned, that burden of guilt...

All human tendencies, the best and the worst, are summed up in each individual... all the affective tendencies; love and hatred; all in one single being...

If, in spite of our inner contradictions, we set out again every morning towards Christ, it is not with any kind of normality in mind. It is with the ultimate goal in view, the goal beyond our hopes, that of becoming conformed to the very likeness of Jesus himself.

Who could condemn, since Christ is risen? He condemns no one; he never punishes...

He is praying in us, offering us the liberation of forgiveness.

—Brother Roger of Taizé

Brother Roger spoke these words for the first time at Easter 1973. I was still young; I had come to Taizé and was in the crowd gathered to celebrate the Resurrection. I remember that many people were deeply touched by these words.

Christ is the manifestation of God's compassion for every human being. The vision of God as a stern judge who condemns has wreaked havoc in many minds. Brother Roger took the opposite tack by saying: All God can do is love. Brother Roger said this very clearly, without adding any conditions or warnings. To many people, he communicated this conviction: You are loved by God as you are; you are close to God forever.

In his youth, he had known Christians who believed the gospel imposed harsh burdens on believers. Because of that, there was a time when faith became difficult for him and when doubts rose in him. Trusting in God was a lifelong struggle for him. But his mother remained a point of reference. She used to say that the words of Saint John, "God is love" (1 John 4:16), were enough for her.

Today, to make the Christian faith accessible to as many people as possible, it is vital to convey what is at the center of the gospel: God's greatness, God's omnipotence revealed as love, as the infinite capacity to come close to humanity. God loves without conditions. It is essential to recall this, especially to a younger generation for whom warnings block the road to discovering a God of love.

DR. SUHAIR HASSAN AL QURASHI

Suhair Hassan Al Qurashi is the president of Dar Al-Hekma College, one of the first and leading private colleges for women in the Kingdom of Saudi Arabia (www.daralhekma.edu.sa). She received a PhD in education and a Master of Philosophy in educational research from Cambridge University, United Kingdom. In addition, Suhair has a Master of Science in management organizational development from United States International University, California. Suhair promotes academic and cultural exchange programs and has given presentations at many conferences including the Interfaith Dialogue Conference at the United Nations, New York, and Muslim Heritage in Our World: Social Cohesion Conference at the Houses of Parliament, United Kingdom.

> . . . My Lord!
> Dispose me always
> to give thanks for Your grace,
> with which You have graced me
> and my parents,
> and that I do righteous deeds
> with which You are pleased.
> And make righteous for me my children.
> Indeed, I have repented to You.
> And, most surely,
> I am of those who are Muslims
> in willing submission to God alone.
>
> —Qur'an 46:15

This verse from the Qur'an expresses the strength and power of the Creator and humbles the reciter as a result.

For me, prayer is the focal point and spiritual essence of every belief system. God, the Creator, established this ritual in all His revelations to mankind. Muslims believe that Islam is the concluding message from God among all revealed religions and recognize that this ritual is an integral part of all of His revelations.

Muslims pray five times a day at prescribed intervals. When doing so, they connect to their beloved Creator in search of peace, strength, and wisdom, hence purifying their souls from sin and alleviating themselves of suffering.

Before sunrise, Muslims start the day with the early-morning prayer, which bestows upon them a sense of comfort and purity that is healing and rejuvenating. Similarly, at noon and in the afternoon, Muslims pray again in order to reenergize. By praying at the end of the day, at sunset and later at night, they complete the cycle of spirituality and cool down from the stresses of the day. All five daily required prayers have a set of specified physical movements, thus enabling the mind to be always alert to what is being recited.

DR. SWEE CHAI ANG

Dr. Swee Ang was raised as a Christian in Singapore. She studied medicine there and in the United Kingdom. Shocked by the suffering of the war victims in Lebanon and Gaza, Swee has committed herself to working in both places periodically since the 1980s. After witnessing the 1982 massacre in Beirut's Sabra and Shatilla Palestinian refugee camps, she testified before the Israeli Kahan Commission. Her book From Beirut to Jerusalem *presents her account of the events she witnessed. A founding member and current patron of the British charity, Medical Aid for Palestinians (MAP), Swee received the Star of Palestine award from the late President Yasser Arafat (www.map-uk.org). Currently, Swee is a consultant orthopedic and trauma surgeon in London.*

> Love never fails. But where there are prophecies, they will cease; where there are tongues, they will be stilled; where there is knowledge, it will pass away. For we know in part and we prophesy in part, but when completeness comes, what is in part disappears. When I was a child, I spoke like a child, I thought like a child, I reasoned like a child; when I became an adult, I put an end to childish ways. For now we see in a mirror, dimly, but then we will see face to face. Now I only know in part; then I will know fully, even as I have been fully known. And now faith, hope and love abide, these three; and the greatest of these is love.
>
> Pursue love and strive for the spiritual gifts...
>
> —1 Corinthians 13:8–10, 11–13, 14:1

In the situation of war and conflicts there are often so many sides. I grew up as a fundamentalist Christian supporting Israel. I was told Arabs were terrorists. In 1982 the British media broadcasted the relentless bombing of Beirut and Lebanon by Israeli planes. Many of those killed and injured were innocent civilians, including children. I could not understand why Israel was doing this. There were heated debates among my Christian and Jewish friends, blaming different parties. I asked God for an answer, for wisdom and understanding. There was no answer for a few weeks. Then I came across this passage from the letter of Paul to the Corinthians. The Apostle Paul called his own understanding childish compared to God's wisdom, but urged us to love. When I read this, I knew that I was only a child and may never understand things fully on this side of heaven. But I was to pursue love. It brought back the commandment of Jesus—"You shall love your neighbor as yourself."

In a flash I understood that God was not going to be impressed with all the debates, knowledge, and commentaries. He wanted me to love. A couple of days later an appeal came from Christian Aid asking for a surgeon to go out to Lebanon to treat the wounded. I resigned from my job in London and flew out to Beirut.

That was twenty-eight years ago. Since then I have seen much suffering. I continue to look after the Palestinians in Lebanon and Gaza. In 2005, in my hospital, the Royal London, I operated on the victims of the July 7th bombing. I was able to be with the people of Pakistan when an earthquake devastated their country. In my prayers I have ceased asking God why there is so much suffering. Instead I ask Him to teach me how to love the people He has put under my care as a Christian should. I will entrust the answers to my "why" for the day of perfection, when I will see Him face to face, when I will know fully.

M. SYAFI'I ANWAR

Born in Indonesia, Syafi'i Anwar is a former journalist committed to religious freedom. After obtaining his PhD in history and political sociology from the University of Melbourne, Australia, he was selected as one of five independent experts by the United Nations High Commissioner for Human Rights representing Asian states. Former executive director of the International Center for Islam and Pluralism, an organization dedicated to promoting democratic, pluralist, tolerant Islam throughout Southeast Asia (www.icipglobal.org), Syafi'i Anwar is currently a senior research fellow in the Indonesia Program at Harvard's John F. Kennedy School of Government. He is dedicated to reforming pesantren *(Islamic boarding schools), promoting pluralism, and countering religious fundamentalism through ODEL (Open, Distance, and E-Learning).*

> We wish to write "battle" on a leaf
> And see that leaf dry up with the fall and
> crumble away.
> We wish to write "anger" on the cloud
> So that it may rain and the clouds disappear.
> We wish to write "hatred" on the snow
> So that the sun may shine and the snow may
> melt away.
> And we wish to write "friendship" and "love" on
> the hearts of newborn babies
> So that friendship and love may grow with them
> and envelop the world.
>
> —Fethullah Gülen

As a human rights activist and defender of pluralism, I am very touched by this poem. It inspires me to have a better understanding and approach in dealing with issues of religious conflict as well as promoting interfaith dialogue and cooperation. It's really the best humanistic approach I have ever practiced in my life and activities.

ZAINAH ANWAR

Zainah Anwar is a founding member and former executive director of Sisters in Islam (SIS), a Malaysian non-governmental organization (NGO) working for women's rights within an Islamic framework (www.sistersinislam.org.my). Now a board member of SIS, Zainah is currently director of Musawah, the SIS-initiated Global Movement for Equality and Justice in the Muslim Family (www.musawah.org). Zainah also writes a monthly column entitled "Sharing the Nation" in The Star, *the largest-circulation English-language daily newspaper in Malaysia. Her book* Islamic Revivalism in Malaysia: Dakwah among the Students *has become a standard reference in the study of Islam in Malaysia.*

Bismillahi Rahmani Rahim (In the name of God,
the Merciful and the Compassionate)

For Muslim men and women,
For believing men and women,
For devout men and women,
For men and women who are patient and
constant,
For men and women who humble themselves,
For men and women who give in charity,
For men and women who fast and deny
themselves,
For men and women who guard their chastity, and
For men and women who engage much in
God's praise,
For them, has God prepared forgiveness and
great reward.

—Qur'an 33:35

This is my favorite verse in the Qur'an as it unequivocally affirms the equality of men and women in their rights and duties as believers, and that God will forgive and reward them both equally.

If women are equal to men before God, why are we then not equal before men? This is the perpetual question Muslim women ask in our struggle to be treated as human beings of equal worth and dignity and our indignation that, in the name of Islam, we are denied our right to equality and just treatment.

I love the context in which the verse was revealed to the Prophet Muhammad (peace be upon him). It is reported that one of his wives, Umm Salama, had questioned the Prophet as to why men were often mentioned in the Qur'an and why women were not, thus giving the impression that God was speaking to men only. One day as Umm Salama sat in her room combing her hair, she heard the Prophet in the mosque next door recite the verse as it was being revealed to him.

I recite this verse often as it affirms to me the justice of Islam. And at Sisters in Islam, we like to read this verse at the opening of some of our public forums. I commissioned a calligrapher to write the script for this verse and it proudly sits framed at the entrance to the SIS office to remind us all that we are equal before God.

IMAM DR. MUHAMMAD NURAYN ASHAFA

Imam Ashafa is an Islamic cleric. He is co-founder and co-director of the Interfaith Mediation Centre in Kaduna, Nigeria, with Pastor Wuye *(see page 204)**, a former religious enemy. The Centre was founded in 1995 and is a faith-based organization responsible for mediating peace between Christians and Muslims (www.imcnigeria.org). Their story is one of triumph and transformation, from hate to love, from vengeance to forgiveness, and from exclusion to inclusion. It has been made into a film,* The Imam and the Pastor. *Imam Ashafa enjoys preaching on Islam.*

Merciful God, You made all of the people of the world in Your own image and placed before us the pathway of salvation through different Preachers who claimed to have been Your Saints and Prophets. But, the contradictions in their teachings and interpretations of them have resulted in creating divisions, hatreds and bloodshed in the world community. Millions of innocent men, women and children have so far been brutally killed by the militants of several religions who have been committing horrifying crimes against humanity, and millions more would be butchered by them in the future, if You do not help us find ways to reunite peacefully.

IN THE NAME OF GOD, THE COMPASSIONATE, THE MERCIFUL,

> look with compassion on the whole human family; take away the controversial teachings of arrogance, divisions and hatreds which have badly infected our hearts; break down the walls that separate us; reunite us in bonds of love; and work through our struggle and confusion to accomplish Your purposes on earth; that, in Your good time, all nations and races may jointly serve You in justice, peace and harmony. Amen.
>
> —Movement for Reforming Society, "Prayer for Unity"

Unity is strength. When the sand grains unite they become a vast desert. When drops of water unite they become a boundless ocean. The conglomeration of stars in the firmament of sky soothes our eyes. The seven colors emerge in the shape of a bewitching rainbow. The unity of people makes an invincible, strong nation. This is the reason Islam lays great stress on the importance of unity. The Islamic concept of Tawhid is the other name for the unity of humankind.

HIS ALL HOLINESS BARTHOLOMEW

Ecumenical Patriarch Bartholomew is spiritual leader to 300 million Orthodox Christians worldwide. He has worked tirelessly for reconciliation among Christian churches and other faith communities, supporting Orthodox countries as they emerged from religious persecution behind the Iron Curtain. His efforts to promote human rights and religious tolerance, together with his pioneering work for international peace and environmental protection, have placed him at the forefront of global visionaries as an apostle of love, peace, and reconciliation (www.patriarchate.org). He has earned the title "Green Patriarch" for his ecological initiatives, and in 2008 he was named one of the world's "100 Most Influential Leaders" by Time *magazine.*

Heavenly King, Comforter, Spirit of Truth.
Present everywhere and filling all things,
Treasury of blessings and giver of life,
Come and abide in us,
And cleanse our hearts of every impurity,
And save our souls,
For you are good and love all people.
—Orthodox Christian prayer

This ancient Christian prayer, recited at the beginning of every formal service in the Orthodox Church and every personal meditation of Orthodox Christians throughout the world, is, after the Lord's Prayer, perhaps one of the most frequently recited prayers in our church. It is also the central prayer of the Feast of Pentecost, the celebration of the light and fire, the divine grace of the Holy Spirit in the heart and in the world.

It has always appealed to us as a discernment and declaration of God's presence "everywhere and in all things" as well as "in us and all people." Over the years, our ministry has sought to underline the beauty and sacredness of all creation, which invites us to respect and protect every detail of the natural environment, to the last speck of dust. Moreover, our ministry has endeavored to highlight and promote the significance of interfaith dialogue, which obliges us to understand and respect every difference in the global society—to the least of our brothers and sisters.

There is a softness and openness to this prayer, which describes the Holy Spirit both as a gentle breeze that inspires simplicity and sensitivity in our lifestyle, as well as a transforming fire that condemns indifference and injustice in our world.

CAMILA BATMANGHELIDJH

Camila Batmanghelidjh is the founder of two children's charities —The Place 2 Be and Kids Company, where Camila currently works with traumatized young people living in London. Set up in 1996, Kids Company provides therapeutic and social work support to 17,000 children through forty-three different sites (www.kidsco.org.uk). A woman of all faiths, Camila trained as a psychotherapist, engaged in eighteen years of psychoanalysis, and has become an advocate for vulnerable children. She is the recipient of many awards and author of Shattered Lives: Children who Live with Courage and Dignity. *Kids Company received the 2007 Liberty and Justice Human Rights Award.*

O God, forgive our rich nation where small
babies die of cold quite legally.
O God, forgive our rich nation where small
children suffer from hunger quite legally.
O God, forgive our rich nation where toddlers
and school children die from guns sold quite
legally.
O God, forgive our rich nation that lets children
be the poorest group of citizens quite
legally.
O God, forgive our rich nation that lets the rich
continue to get more at the expense of the
poor quite legally.
O God, forgive our rich nation, which thinks
security rests in missiles rather than in
mothers, and in bombs rather than in babies.

O God, forgive our rich nation for not giving You sufficient thanks by giving to others their daily bread.
O God, help us never to confuse what is quite legal with what is just and right in Your sight.
—Marian Wright Edelman

I love this prayer because it eloquently expresses the tragedy of childhood maltreatment in Britain. Although Britain is very rich, it is at the bottom of the league of the wealthiest nations for children's welfare. Britain locks up more children and young people than any European country, but 80 percent reoffend post-custody. Annually, 1.5 million children are abused and neglected; at least sixty-four children are sexually abused in England and Wales every day. Child poverty figures are also shocking.

The statistics presented here are confirmed by many sources, including the National Society for the Prevention of Cruelty to Children—NSPCC. The crime sustaining such degeneration in the care of children is mindlessness. The government does not set out to actively harm children, but it does so through apathy and policies that lack vision. The abused child cannot hold society accountable; neither can she/he protest through the media. So, since Victorian times, Britain has appeared as a nation that cares for its vulnerable children because we follow procedures and policies. I pray that this betrayal stops.

THE REVEREND MARTA BENAVIDES

Marta Benavides was born and raised in El Salvador. She was responsible for setting up the first refugee centers, and for much of the humanitarian work organized by Archbishop Oscar Romero, who died a martyr in 1980 during El Salvador's civil war. Throughout this armed conflict (1980–1992), Marta worked nationally and internationally for a peaceful solution, which was eventually achieved through United Nations peace accords. As leader of the Global Movement for Culture of Peace, Marta works ecumenically and with secular groups educating people for a culture of peace. Committed to social transformation, Marta's focus is on peaceful relations with all humanity and care for Mother Earth (www.museoaja.org).

Pray then like this:
Our Father who art in heaven,
Hallowed is thy name.
Thy kingdom come,
Thy will be done,
On earth as it is in heaven.
Give us this day our daily bread;
And forgive us our debts,
As we also have forgiven our debtors;
And lead us not into temptation,
But deliver us from evil.
—The Lord's Prayer (Matthew 6:9–13)

The Lord's Prayer appears in the Bible, the sacred book for all Christians around the world, as it was taught by our Brother Jesus, to be in communion with Our Father. For me, it is the most important and symbolic prayer. It also affirms all of Jesus' teachings. I call it the Our Father and Mother Prayer, in order to recognize both the Father and Mother presence in the Creator Spirit, and I recite it now as an affirmation, not as a wish nor as a request, but in recognition that all has been given to us already by the Great Spirit.

> Our Father-Mother who are in heaven, hallowed is thy name
> Your kingdom is. Your will is done, on earth as it is in heaven,
> You give us each day our daily bread and I work to make sure we all enjoy it.
> You have forgiven us, since the beginning.
> We have never had any debts, so no one owes me anything.
> You never lead us into temptation, but you give us a life that challenges us to grow in wisdom and grace, thus you do not have to deliver us from evil, for you are my and our light, if I so choose it, thus no evil is in my path and life.
> For, I am in you as you are in me. And so it is.

This prayer, and the way I understand it, is fundamental to how I lead my life and ministry, understand my relationship with the Higher Spirit, and understand how the Higher Spirit relates to humanity. Therefore, my ministry is about a responsible, caring relationship with each other, Mother Earth, and the Divine Being.

This prayer affirms the "how and why" we are on earth; how we must go about manifesting God's will here "*on earth as it is in heaven.*" I affirm that this is our call and challenge—to discern and manifest God's will in real time and intentionally here on earth.

Check Out Receipt

Saline District Library (SDL)
734-429-5450
http://salinelibrary.org
Tuesday, November 06, 2012 7:23:04 PM

Item: 34604910868883
Title: A world of prayer : spiritual leaders, activists, and humanitarians share their favorite prayers
Due: 12/4/2012

Total Items: 1

Stay informed!
Sign up for @the Library e-News
at http://salinelibrary.org

PAULUS BERENSOHN

A spiritually eclectic soul, Paulus Berensohn is inspired by insights and images from Quakerism, Judaism, Buddhism, Daoism, and the Sufi poets; by the movement arts and most especially by the sensuous reciprocity of the animate cosmos. He is a dancer, ceramic artist, journal-maker and keeper, and a poet. A passionate Deep Ecologist with a mystical connection to craft materials and processes, Paulus offers workshops that inspire people to re-imagine their sense of awe and mystery. He lives in North Carolina near the Penland School of Crafts with which he has had a long association. He practices his "old-man dancing" for two pre-dawn hours every day.

> Oh, what a catastrophe, what a maiming of love when it was made a personal, merely personal feeling, taken away from the rising and the setting of the sun, and cut off from the magic connection of the solstice and equinox! This is what is the matter with us. We are bleeding at the roots because we are cut off from the earth and sun and stars, and love is a grinning mockery, because, poor blossom, we plucked it from its stem on the tree of Life, and expected it to keep on blooming in our civilized vase on the table…
>
> It is a question, practically, of relationship. We must get back into relation, vivid and nourishing relation to the cosmos and the universe. The way is through daily ritual, and the re-awakening …the ritual of dawn and noon and sunset, the ritual of kindling fire and pouring water…
>
> —D. H. Lawrence

I was thrilled and encouraged by these evocative words of D. H. Lawrence when I came across them some decades ago. They fuelled and continue to empower my passion for the behavior of art for, like love, art reconnects me, again and again, to rituals of relationship and participation, with a more than just human world, to a deeper, aesthetic and somatic ecology.

As a dancer and as an artist who works with the primary materials of the craft arts, with movement, with breath and energy, with fire and water, with clay and fiber, with wood, metals and paper—these materials all have rich lives of their own that carry creation stories that inspire and draw me closer.

Love is healing, art is healing. Art is not a noun, but a verb. Not objects but soul's love affair with the building blocks of continuous creation, the stream of living things.

Lawrence speaks to our deracinated being, to our loss of rootedness. "Take off your shoes," I imagine him whispering between the lines to my inner ear. "You are standing on holy ground: earth your feet, your feet of clay. Allow the energy of the earth and the current of the cosmos to marry in you, so that the artist you are, that we all are, can sing up the earth, sing up the sun and the moon!"

FR. DANIEL BERRIGAN, SJ

Poet, playwright, teacher and priest, Fr. Daniel Berrigan is a renowned peace activist. A founding member of the 1980s Plowshares Movement, an anti-nuclear weapons movement, he committed many acts of civil disobedience. Between 1970 and 1995, Fr. Berrigan spent nearly seven years in prison for protest-related offences, including the public burning of Vietnam War draft files from a Catonsville, Maryland, office. His many awards include the 1988 Thomas Merton Award and the 1998 Jesuit Campion Medal. He has worked with cancer and AIDS patients in New York City, where he now lives in a community of priests.

O WISDOM OF GOD MOST HIGH, WHO GUIDES CREATION WITH POWER AND LOVE, COME, TEACH US TO WALK IN THE PATH OF KNOWLEDGE.

The first day is the day of relief.

Relief from chaos, double mindedness, the blocked heart, the unburned bridges. Relief from the no-person land between yes and no. From the impasse of maybe. Jesus is the Yes of God (2 Corinthians 1:20). These wounds are healed.

O LEADER AND LOVER, COME RESCUE US WITH YOUR MIGHTY POWER.

This is the day named winter.

Root and branch, the sap is stilled. Root and branch, it will flow again.

This is the day of patience and relief from the inhuman machines and machinations of this world.

O KEY OF DAVID, WHO OPENS THE GATES OF GOD'S REALM, COME, FREE THOSE WHO SIT IN PRISON AND THE SHADOW OF DEATH.

The day of promise.

To some, the earth is a dungeon, a theater of cruelty, a slave market, a mortuary.

To others, the earth is a task; make of it a holy dwelling place, a door, a garden. There, a wedding banquet is in progress.

Open the door, to ourselves and others.

Shout it; the promise, the invitation. Come in, each and all.

O RADIANT DAWN, SPLENDOR, SUN OF JUSTICE, COME, ILLUMINE THOSE WHO ARE LOST IN THE SHADOW OF DEATH.

The fourth day dawns. It is the equinox, night no longer rules.

This day brings also the flame within, to that combustible matter named soul.

In Christ, our lives proffer light.

O FLOWER OF JESSE, SIGN OF GOD'S LOVE FOR ALL PEOPLE, COME, SAVE US WITHOUT DELAY.

The fifth day is the day of mindfulness, and of mindful words.

Our lips have been touched, and our hearts too.

We have touched that realm which is beyond words, the realm of tears.

O HOPE OF ALL NATIONS, COME, SAVE THOSE YOU HAVE CREATED WITH YOUR TWO HANDS.

This is the day of dance.

Like god Shiva, we are created with a hundred arms that weave a thousand gestures; freedom, exaltation, beckoning and grief.

Our hands are empty; the dancer is vulnerable.

O EMMANUEL, GOD WITH US, COME, SAVE US, CHRIST OUR GOD.

The seventh day, and the eighth.

This is the time of rest, deep and steady.

Deep as slumber, awake as the thousand-eyed Buddha.

On this day we breathe deep, and are silent.
We hear it said; all shall be well.

—Daniel Berrigan, SJ
Reflections on the "O Antiphons"

DR. PUSHPA BHARDWAJ-WOOD

Pushpa Bhardwaj-Wood, a Hindu, was born and brought up in India before moving to New Zealand in 1980. She has a PhD in Indian religions and works at the Retirement Commission as a senior education advisor. Pushpa's involvement in interfaith activities began during her childhood in India and has continued since her arrival in New Zealand. She is a founding member of both the interfaith movement in New Zealand and the Wellington Interfaith Group and has participated in many Asia-Pacific Interfaith forums (www.interfaith.org.nz). Her passion and lifelong dream is to utilize religion as a uniting force for humanity.

O Supreme Lord!
Thou art ever existent,
Ever conscious, ever blissful.
We meditate on Thy most adorable glory.
Mayest Thou guide and inspire our intellect
On the path of highest divinity!
May we be able to discriminate
Between truth and falsehood.

—Rigveda, 3.62.10

I was brought up in the Brahmin caste, in a deeply religious household with very forward-thinking parents. Exposed to all the major faith traditions, I had a privileged childhood listening to visiting scholars and religious leaders, given opportunities to ask questions and the freedom to choose how to worship.

From an early age, I had access to and was fascinated by the *Vedas* and *Shri mad Bhagavad Gita.* Although this passage above is attributed to a Hindu text, its message of omnipresence is universal and can be found in many other religious traditions. This favorite prayer best summarizes my understanding of the Hindu philosophy and gives me strength and direction in my path of discovering the ultimate truth and in my daily quest for Moksha (freedom from the cycle of birth and rebirth and salvation)!

LEONARDO BOFF

Leonardo Boff is a prominent Brazilian liberation theologian. He was ordained a Franciscan priest but his theological outspokenness and political activism for social justice caused controversy within the Church, leading to his resignation in 1992. Leonardo is a professor of theology and spirituality at universities in Brazil, Germany, and the United States. In addition to co-editing the Earth Charter, he is the author of more than eighty books, including Jesus Christ Liberator; Church, Charism and Power; Cry of the Earth, Cry of Poor; *and* The Tao of Liberation: Exploring the Ecology of Transformation.

My dear, great Mother and Common House! You were born slowly, after millions and millions of years, pregnant with creative energy.

Your body, made of cosmic powder, was a seed in the belly of the great red stars that, after exploding, threw you into unlimited space. You came in a nest, like an embryo, in the heart of an ancestral star, in the center of the Milky Way, then transformed into a Super Nova. The Super Nova also succumbed to such splendor and exploded. You came to a stop in the welcoming breast of a Nebula where, already a grown girl, you wandered in search of a home. And the Nebula itself transformed into a splendid Sun of light and heat: our Sun.

He fell in love with you, was attracted to you and wanted you in his house; your planet, along with Mars, Mercury, Venus and other companions. And the Sun celebrated a spousal relationship with you. Of your marriage with the Sun were born sons and daughters, fruits of your unlimited fertility, from the very tiniest bacteria, virus and fungi to the largest and most complex plants, fish and animals. And as a noble expression of the history of the life, you generated us, men and women, to be of conscience, of intelligence and of love.

As you are humans, you are Land, the part of you that feels, thinks, loves and cares. And you continue growing, although adult, for inside the universe is the breast of the God-Father-and-Mother of infinite tenderness. He came and for him we return for complete fullness that only you can grant us. They will want, God-Father-and-Mother, to dive into you and be with you forever along with the Land.

And now, dear Land, I feel that I am a universal priest. I am going to carry out the will of Jesus in the force of his Spirit. As he, full of unction, I take you in my impure hands, to pronounce to you the sacred Word that the universe guards and you are going to hear:

"*Hoc est corpus meum*: This is my body. *Hoc est sanguis meus*: This is my blood."

And then I felt: what was Land was transformed into Paradise and what was human life itself transformed into divine life. What was bread became body of God and what was wine became sacred blood.

Finally, Land, with your sons and daughters, you arrived as God. Finally home forever. "Do this in my memory."

For this, from time to time, I fulfill your mandate. I pronounce your essential word, dear Land, about all of the universe. And along with it and with you we feel the Body of God, in the full splendor of your glory.

—Leonardo Boff

FAOLE BOKOI

Faole Bokoi lives in Manari village, near the Kokoda Track in Papua New Guinea. Born before Christianity came to the village, Faole is one of three surviving Kokoda Track "Fuzzy Wuzzy Angels," so named for their essential services to Australian soldiers during the Kokoda campaign of World War II and for their frizzy hair. Faole assisted the sick and wounded, carrying food and medical supplies amidst the harsh terrain, receiving no payment but for food and tobacco. After the war, Faole became a policeman, a magistrate, and later a respected village court chairman totally committed to peace. Faole is a Seventh Day Adventist.

> Yea, though I walk through the valley of the
> shadow of death, I will fear no evil:
> For thou art with me; thy rod and thy staff they
> comfort me.
> Surely goodness and mercy shall follow me all
> the days of my life: and I will dwell in the
> house of the Lord for ever.
>
> —Psalm 23:4, 6

Once again, I am happy I have done my part in the victory and peace we can share today. I continue to tell my children, my grandchildren, my great-grandchildren and my people to maintain this spirit of unity and to keep the peace. I am very proud that the Kokoda Track has become a living symbol of peace for so many years.

My prayer for the community is to always live peacefully, respectably, joyfully, lovingly, and honestly.

THE REVEREND DR. MARCUS BRAYBROOKE

Marcus Braybrooke is a parish priest who has worked as an interfaith activist for forty years. He is president of the World Congress of Faiths, a Peace Councillor, and co-founder of the Three Faiths Forum (www.worldfaiths.org). In addition, he is the author of more than forty books, including Learn to Pray, Beacons of the Light, *and the compilation* 1,000 World Prayers.

May the Spirit of Silence open our hearts to
God's transforming love;
May the Spirit of Compassion help us to feel
for the sufferings of others;
May the Spirit of Love melt the cold hearts of
those who trample on human rights;
May the Spirit of Beauty teach us to treasure
Mother Earth;
May the Spirit of Wisdom help us to learn
from spiritual teachers of every faith;
May the Spirit of Patience and Endurance
strengthen the oppressed
and those who are exiled from their homes;
May the Spirit of Courage strengthen
those who speak for those
whose voice is never heard;
May the Spirit of Non-violence bring healing,
peace and justice
to those who live in countries torn apart
by conflict;

May the Spirit of Unity help us to welcome
people of every country
and creed as brothers and sisters.
—Marcus Braybrooke

This is an adaptation of a prayer that I wrote for the people of Tibet, but it applies more widely. Indeed, I hope it has a universal resonance. The prayer expresses my aspirations, from which I fall far short, and my major concerns—in addition to care for family members.

THE REVEREND ERNESTO CARDENAL

One of the original voices of liberation theology, Ernesto Cardenal is a revolutionary Nicaraguan priest, poet, and sculptor renowned for speaking out for justice and freedom in Latin America. Ordained a priest in 1965, Ernesto actively supported the Sandinista revolution that overthrew President Somoza in 1979 and was briefly Nicaraguan Minister of Culture in the Sandinista government. He is famous for conveying the Nicaraguan struggle to every reader of his poetry. In his book Salmos *(Psalms), the poems express the tension between his revolutionary political fervor and his religious faith. A Nobel Prize nominee in literature, Ernesto lives and works in Managua.*

Lord listen to what I'm saying
hear my cries
and my I-can't-stand-it
You never plot with dictators
your politics are straight
They don't fool you with slick campaigns
you're not behind them
the con-men
the party bosses

Their words are dead
you know there's nothing in them
their press-releases and statements

Their speeches are honeyed with peace
they drip love and kindness
and their stock-piles grow the faster

They hold peace conferences
more they could not
They talk of friendship among nations
In secret they prepare weapons of war
of utter destruction

Their wavelengths dance with lies
evil songs in the darkness
Their desks are heavy with plots
Lord preserve me from their scheming

Their mouths are machine-guns
and their tongues deal death
Punish them Lord
Make dust of their projects
and cheap ideas
of all their memoranda

When the siren wails the last warning
you will be with me
You will be my refuge
my strength and deep shelter

You will bless the man
who shuns their slogans and campaigns
their hand-outs and all they say
You will circle him with armor
and shield him with all your love

—Ernesto Cardenal,
Hear My Cries: Psalm 5

DR. SHEILA CASSIDY

Sheila Cassidy was educated both in England and Australia and studied medicine at Sydney University. She achieved "fame but no fortune" for being detained and tortured in Chile after having treated a wounded revolutionary at the beginning of the Pinochet regime. On her return to England, she became an outspoken advocate for human rights and wrote the international bestseller Audacity to Believe. *After two years in a convent, Sheila worked with cancer patients for twenty years and now works part-time as a psychotherapist in Plymouth, England.*

There is room in the world for loving;
 there is no room for hate.
There is room in the world for sharing;
 there is no room for greed.
There is room for justice;
 no room for privilege.
There is room for compassion;
 no room for pride.
The world is ample enough for the needs of all;
 too small for the greed of a few.
Let us learn that we depend on each other;
 that the eye cannot say to the hand
 "I need you not."
Let us be delicate with persons.
Let us touch the earth lightly with hands like
 petals.
Let us speak softly and carry no stick.
Let us open the clenched fist and extend the
 open palm.

Let us mourn till others are comforted,
    weep till others laugh.
Let us be sleepless till all can sleep untroubled.
Let us be meek till all stand up in pride.
Let us be frugal till all are filled.
Let us give till all have received.
Let us make no claims till all have had their due.
Let us be slaves till all are free.
Let us lay down our lives
    till others have life abundantly.
Let us be restless for others, serene within
    ourselves.
Let us be as gods.

—John Harriott, SJ

John was a Jesuit priest who left the Society to marry. I find this poem "Our World" (from which I have taken this extract) pure gospel. It sums up exactly what I believe and how I try to live.

ARCHBISHOP ELIAS CHACOUR

Archbishop Elias Chacour, a Greek Melkite Catholic, was born in 1939 to a Christian family in the Palestinian village of Biram, a village entirely made up of Christians. After the ethnic cleansing that accompanied the establishment of Israel, Elias and his family along with many others became refugees in their own country and lived in extreme poverty. He later studied in Paris and was ordained a priest in Nazareth in 1965. In 1982, he created and is now president of Mar Elias Educational Institutions in Ibillim, Galilee (www.pilgrimsofibillin.org). In 2006, Archbishop Elias was elected the Melkite Catholic archbishop of Galilee.

> Seeing the crowds, he went onto the mountain. And when he was seated his disciples came to him. Then he began to speak. This is what he taught them:
>
> How blessed are the poor in spirit: the kingdom of Heaven is theirs.
> Blessed are the gentle: they shall have the earth as inheritance.
> Blessed are those that mourn: they shall be comforted.
> Blessed are those who hunger and thirst for uprightness: they shall have their fill.
> Blessed are the merciful: they shall have mercy shown them.
> Blessed are the poor in heart: they shall see God.
>
> —Matthew 5:1–8

One of the most striking passages of the Bible for me would be these first eight verses of the Sermon on the Mount (Mathew 5:1–8). It is not about blessings or beatitudes, it is rather an urgent calling from the Lord to his disciples to get up, to move, to do something if they are really and truly hungry and thirsty for righteousness or for justice.

The same goes for the other verses and very especially for the one that calls us to be peacemakers (verse 9). We do not need or rather we need not be contemplators of peace but builders of peace, proactive for peace.

These verses are an introduction to the main, central revelation the Lord wanted to make, which consists of revealing the extraordinary secret, or rather, mystery, which says: "In Heaven we have a Father and to him we should pray ultimately: Our Father in Heaven, hallowed be Your Name" (Matthew 6:9).

The rest of the Sermon on the Mount leads us to become more and more aware of the importance of our relations with that God-Father in Heaven.

VANNATH CHEA, MPA

Vannath Chea is a prominent sociologist in Cambodia. She has a Master's degree in Public Administration and is a former president of the Centre for Social Development, a non-governmental organization advocating the institutionalization of democratic values and principles. Vannath served on the special mission of the United Nations Transitional Authority in Cambodia (UNTAC) in 1992–1993, contributing to rehabilitation and reconciliation. A nominee in a group of one thousand women for the Nobel Peace Prize in 2005, Vannath is currently senior advisor to the Girl Guides Association of Cambodia.

The first truth states there is suffering—get to
  know it!
The second truth states that suffering is caused
  by mental attachment—abandon it!
The third truth is that cessation of attachment
  brings end of suffering—realize it!
The fourth truth suggests a way of life by which
  self-centered attachment (and so suffering)
  is reduced—practice it!

This is expressed as Eight Steps of the Path:
1) right views, 2) right thought, 3) right speech,
4) right conduct, 5) right efforts, 6) right
mindfulness, 7) right concentration, and
8) right livelihood.

—John A. McConnell

During the tragic rule of the Khmer Rouge from 1975 to 1979, approximately 5 million people out of 8 million were displaced and an estimated 1.7 million died from killings, disease, and starvation. One time I was so exhausted, I felt that I was about to die. I silently prayed for mercy from Buddha, Dharma [*cosmic law*], and Sangha [*community of monks*] and after a while I became serene and calm.

Many of my family either died or went missing. Even after thirty years, I am still looking for my missing brother. Leaving my parents behind, I fled Cambodia and lived in refugee camps in Thailand and the Philippines, attaining refugee status to resettle in the United States in 1981. I returned to Cambodia in 1992 to join the UNTAC Mission and have lived here ever since.

Understanding the Four Noble Truths guides me through life's turbulence. Pol Pot, the master of the "Killing Fields," died from natural causes in 1998. In 2002, I went to the place where he was cremated and, with equanimity and no hard feelings, lit a candle and prayed for the liberation of his soul. I believe that Pol Pot's existence in this world is the law of nature. War and peace, life and death, sorrow and joy, good and evil, disaster and harmony are intertwined. That is the law of nature. That is life!

I cannot pick and choose the things that I like and discard things that I do not like. But what I can do is maintain my mental balance and equilibrium to better face the reality and be part of the solution.

SISTER JOAN D. CHITTISTER, OSB

Sister Joan Chittister is a Benedictine nun and founder and executive director of Benetvision, a resource and research center for contemporary spirituality (www.benetvision.org). She is co-chair of the Global Peace Initiative of Women, a partner organization of the United Nations, facilitating a worldwide network of women peace builders. Sr. Joan is an international lecturer and award-winning author of more than forty books, including The Gift of Years: Growing Older Gracefully *and* Welcome to the Wisdom of the World. *She has received numerous awards for her work for justice, peace, and equality, especially for women in the Church and in society. She was prioress of her Benedictine community for twelve years.*

I bow to the one who signs the cross.
I bow to the one who sits with the Buddha.
I bow to the one who wails at the wall.
I bow to the OM flowing in the Ganges.
I bow to the one who faces Mecca,
    whose forehead touches holy ground.
I bow to dervishes whirling in mystical wind.
I bow to the north,
    to the south,
    to the east,
    to the west.
I bow to the God within each heart.
I bow to epiphany,
    to God's face revealed.
I bow. I bow. I bow.

—Sr. Mary Lou Kownacki, OSB

I chose this prayer because it points us all to the awareness that it is an enlightening excursion, this wandering into the spiritual insights of other whole cultures, other whole intuitions of the spiritual life, and other whole traditions of holy ones. It depends for its fruitfulness on openness of heart and awareness of mind. But the journey is well worth the exertion it takes to see old ideas in new ways because it can bring us to the very height and depth of ourselves. It can even bring fresh hearing and new meaning to the stories that come down to us through our own tradition.

My prayer is that those who make the journey become aware of our God and our world in whole new ways, for that is the one great task of life. May the effect of saying such a prayer be an enlightening one. May it awaken in you that which is deeper than fact, truer than thought, and full of faith. May it remind us all that in every human event and culture and history and revelation is a particle of the Divine to which we turn for meaning in this life, to which we tend for fullness of life hereafter.

BHIKSHUNI THUBTEN CHODRON

Ordained in 1977, Bhikshuni Thubten Chodron is an American nun in the Tibetan Buddhist tradition. Founder and abbess of Sravasti Abbey, a Tibetan monastic community in the United States, she teaches Buddhist philosophy, psychology, and meditation worldwide. She also engages in interfaith dialogue and teaches Buddhism to prisoners. Thubten is the author of several books, including Buddhism for Beginners *and* Working with Anger *(www.sravasti.org and www.thubtenchodron.org).*

Unruly beings are as unlimited as space:
They cannot possibly all be overcome.
But if I overcome thoughts of anger alone,
This will be equivalent to vanquishing all foes.

Where would I possibly find enough leather
With which to cover the surface of the earth?
But wearing leather just on the soles of my shoes
Is equivalent to covering the earth with it.

Likewise, it is not possible for me
To restrain the external course of things;
But should I restrain this mind of mine
What would be the need to restrain all else?

–Shantideva

These verses remind me that our mind/heart—not external people, possessions, or situations—is the source of our happiness and suffering. Instead of trying to change everyone and everything to make them the way I want them to be, it is wiser and more effective to change my mind, freeing it from clinging attachment, anger, and self-centeredness. While we may physically try to do away with our enemies—which is an extremely difficult and dangerous task—new ones will appear. But if we protect our mind from anger, we stop creating the causes that make others want to harm us. And even if they do harm us, we do not get caught up in fear and suspicion, but remain calm and capable of dealing with the situation compassionately.

Trying to change the world and the beings in it so that they conform to our notion of what they should be, so that we will be happy, does not work. People do not want to be controlled and in any case, we cannot go into their minds and make them think and act differently. The one thing that we can manage is our own interpretations, emotions, and reactions. When we apply the antidotes the Buddha and other spiritual teachers taught, we can tame our own minds/hearts to bring peace to ourselves and others.

FR. BOYET CONCEPCION

A priest for more than twenty-seven years, Fr. Boyet has spent his entire ministry helping vulnerable fellow Filipinos. His connections with the poor began in 1982 with a series of "gut-level" encounters where he met and saw the Lord. His meeting with Mother Teresa was also inspirational to him and some locals call him "the barefoot miracle worker." Immersing himself in desperate conditions, he inspires countless benefactors to contribute seed money, building materials, and food for the poor. Facilities include a home for the ailing elderly, a center for the drug addicted, runaways, and emotionally disturbed youths, and an orphanage called the House and Treasure of St. Martin de Porres.

Dear Jesus

Help me to spread Your fragrance everywhere
I go.
Flood my soul with Your spirit and life.
Penetrate and possess my whole being
so utterly that
all my life may only be a radiance of Yours.
Shine through me and be so in me that every
soul I come in contact with
may feel Your presence in my soul.

Let them look up and see no longer me but only
Jesus!
Stay with me and then I shall begin to shine as
You shine,
so to shine as to be a light to others;

The light, O JESUS, will be all from You;
none of it will be mine:
It will be You shining on others through me.
Let me thus praise You in the way You love best:
by shining on those around me.
Let me preach You without preaching,
not by words, but by example,
by the catching force, the sympathetic influence
of what I do,
the evident fullness of the love my heart bears
for You.
Amen.

—John Henry Cardinal Newman

This prayer captures and crystallizes the desire of my heart, that is, to mirror Christ to others through the works of compassion and love. We are channels of that love: what a wonderful privilege and grace. What is faith without works of charity and mission work? And what is this without the poor we serve? The poor are God's treasures, people of dearest value to us. We are channels of that love. What a wonderful privilege and grace!

VENERABLE ROBINA COURTIN

Robina Courtin was ordained a Buddhist nun in the late 1970s. Since then Robina has worked with the Foundation for the Preservation of the Mahayana Tradition, the worldwide network of Tibetan Buddhist activities of her teachers Lama Thubten Yeshe and Lama Zopa Rinpoche. Robina has served as editorial director of Wisdom Publications, editor of Mandala *magazine, executive director of Liberation Prison Project, and as a touring teacher of Buddhism. Her life and work with prisoners have been featured in the documentary films* Chasing Buddha *and* Key to Freedom.

May I purify the power of karma,
May I crush the powers of delusion,
May I render powerless the powerful *maras*
[demons],
And may I perfect the powers of sublime ways.

May I purify an ocean of realms,
May I liberate an ocean of sentient beings,
May I see an ocean of truths,
And may I realize an ocean of wisdom.

May I perform an ocean of perfect deeds,
May I perfect an ocean of prayers,
May I revere an ocean of buddhas,
And may I practice untiringly for an ocean
of eons...

Limitless is the extent of space,
Limitless is the number of sentient beings,

And limitless is the karma and delusions of beings,
Such are the limits of my aspirations.

—Excerpt from "The Great King of Prayers"
from the Avatamsaka Sutra

These are just a few of the sixty-plus stanzas of a prayer expressing the aspirations of the *bodhisattva*, one who devotes this and countless future lives to the welfare of others. I love the vastness of these aspirations, the courage to think limitlessly.

FR. PAOLO DALL'OGLIO, SJ

Italian born Paolo Dall'Oglio lives at the ancient Monastery Deir Mar Musa el-Habashi in the mountain desert near Nebek, Syria. In 1984, committed to building Islamic-Christian harmony, Paolo graduated with a degree in Arabic and Islamic civilization and was ordained a Jesuit priest in the Syriac Catholic Church in Damascus. He initiated restoration of the monastery by organizing work and prayer summer camps for youth. Awarded a PhD on Qur'anic Eschatology and Islamic-Christian dialogue, Paolo moved permanently to Deir Mar Musa in 1991 to establish a monastic community that thrives today (www.deirmarmusa.org). His awards include the 2006 Anna Lindh Euro-Mediterranean Foundation Award for Dialogue Between Cultures.

> Christ, Isa Son of Mary, forgive me, the sinner,
> and have mercy on us.
>
> —Prayer of an Islamic-Christian Heart

The Prayer of the Heart (or of the Name of Jesus) can be traced back to the early Christian communities. It is a type of oriental rosary. Muslims have their own "rosary," related to the ninety-nine names of God, *Allah*, used as well for other kinds of *dhikr* (remembrance of God), formulas that continually remember the divine mystery.

As a Christian committed to interreligious dialogue and harmony-building, I aim to deepen communion with Muslims and Jews when addressing a*l-Masîh*, the Messiah, Christ, source of reconciliation and hope for the children of Abraham.

The words "Isa (Jesus) Son of Mary" are not only a Qur'anic expression, but also an invitation to pray with the heart of Mary. In the Orthodox and Catholic awareness alike, Mary of Nazareth is the starting point and the model of a new humanity. In the Islamic tradition, she is the "chosen" woman. Those who meditate the Prayer of the Heart find in Mary an anchor that helps them bear in their heart the infinite intercession of Isa-Jesus.

Saying "Forgive *me*" helps me become aware of my personal responsibility in the death of Jesus and in violence suffered by sisters and brothers in all times. He knows I need him to volunteer in offering himself and to show the extent of God's love for me, the sinner.

And I say "the sinner" without knowing anymore who is speaking: is it I invoking mercy, for I am aware of my failings, my betrayal, the disease of my ego which causes every holy thing to decay? And I do not really know any longer if it is him, my rabbi and sheikh, in his humanity who in me descends into hell to seek me, the deaf and dumb. From my depths, he cries to his divinity, tragically united to the disaster of his humanity and yet never separated from the Lord, the Father—One with Him and the Spirit in the love of humans. In me, his humanity cries to his divinity.

And he has mercy on us. Who? The One, the Merciful, the Compassionate, Allah, the Father, present in the Son to make us children fully participant in divine communion. How could this separate me from the prayer of my Muslim brothers and sisters and from all my brethren in humanity, and, so to speak, in divinity?

MARIAMA DE LYS WALET MOHAMED

Mariama was born in Timbuktu, Mali. She has managed a travel agency for more than fifteen years, bringing foreigners to the ageless lands of Mali and the Sahara. Mariama enjoys planning and promoting unique journeys to Mali and to other parts of West Africa. Through her work, she stays in close contact with her culture, although she is often confronted with global issues. Her work gives her a deep commitment to quality travels and a profound respect for diversity and humanity (www.touringmali.com).

Desert, my desert, I do not simply like you nor
do I casually speak about you.
I will always love you and promise never to run
away from the heat and the cold.
I am not gathering with those who see you as an
orphan star from ancient times.
My flesh and bones will prove the dunes until
the white sands claim them back.
Traveler and Djinns of the Sahara, help me
gather its rocks to build the oasis
Where I will rest and close my eyes forever as
the sun comes down.

—Mariama De Lys Walet Mohamed

My dream has always been to go back to the desert and enjoy its quiet life and the serenity that surrounds this unique place on earth. So far, the path of my life has taken me away from Mali to the mist of Ireland and to the beaches of Senegal. And as a "modern woman" I cannot envision returning to my birth place of Timbuktu for now, as I look after a business, support a husband who is a world traveler, and care for three children attending schools in the United States, France, and Switzerland.

Fortunately, my husband, also from a diverse cultural background spanning France, India, and Mali, truly enjoys desert life too, from which—as he often says—three main religions emerged as a testimony that God reveals himself only in the silence of the desert! In writing such poems, I keep the dream alive to return to this peaceful and spiritual environment.

FR. JOHN DEAR, SJ

John Dear's work for peace and nonviolence is internationally known. A Jesuit priest, activist, and lecturer, he is the author/editor of twenty-five books, including A Persistent Peace, The Questions of Jesus, Jesus the Rebel, The God of Peace, Transfiguration, *and* Peace Behind Bars. *He has organized hundreds of anti-war demonstrations and been arrested many times in acts of nonviolent civil disobedience at United States military installations (www.johndear.org). Recently, Archbishop Desmond Tutu nominated him for the Nobel Peace Prize.*

> You have heard that it was said, "You shall love your neighbor and hate your enemy." But I say to you, love your enemies, and pray for those who persecute you, that you may be children of your heavenly Father, for he makes his sun rise on the bad and the good, and causes rain to fall on the just and the unjust.
>
> —Matthew 5:43–45

These are the most political, revolutionary words in the entire Bible. To be a Christian, to be a human being, not only means resisting war and nuclear weapons; for Jesus, it means loving the people declared expendable by our governments. We are commanded here to love everyone everywhere with an unconditional, nonviolent, universal love. We no longer support the killing of enemies or preparations to kill. We are summoned to be people of active nonviolence. I find this so exciting and hopeful!

But what is so shocking to me is the reason why we are to love our enemies. Jesus does not say, "Love your enemies because it's the right thing to do, because it's the moral position to take, or because it's the only practical solution left for the world"—even though each of those reasons is correct. He says love your enemies because God loves God's enemies and you are children of the God who practices universal love.

This is the best description of God, of the nature of divinity, in the entire Bible, and it goes against everything we have been taught. The scandal of Christianity is that God is nonviolent. God lets the sun and the rain fall on everyone; we must do the same with our nonviolent love. If we do, we become like our loving God; indeed, we become God's beloved sons and daughters. This is who we are called to be. This is who we already are: God's beloved sons and daughters. And so, we work for the abolition of war, poverty, nuclear weapons, and global warming, and we practice God's universal love, nonviolence, and peace. This is the meaning of life in a nutshell!

VENERABLE DHAMMANANDA BHIKKHUNI

Dhammananda was born Chatsuman Kabilsingh. After her 2001 ordination, she was formally known as Venerable Dhammananda, Thailand's first fully ordained Theravada Buddhist bhikkhuni *(female Buddhist monastic). In 2004, Dhammananda received the Outstanding Buddhist Woman Award from the United Nations and in 2005 she was among the one thousand women nominated for the Nobel Peace Prize. She has had more than thirty years of professorial teaching experience in Buddhism in Thailand and is the author of more than seventy books on subjects including the history of Buddhism and women in Buddhism. A tireless crusader for women's ordination, Dhammananda is abbess of Songdhammakalyani Monastery, the first monastery for* bhikkhunis *in Thailand (www.thaibhikkhunis.org).*

May all sentient beings be happy,
May all sentient beings be free from suffering,
May there be food for the poor,
May there be kindness among the rich,
May there be light of wisdom for the ignorant.
May there be righteousness among the
politicians.
May women realize their own strength,
May the four-fold Buddhists be completed.

—Buddhist prayer and
Venerable Dhammananda's
own words

This is a general Buddhist prayer, but the second half is very much my own as I realize that many of the obstacles to recognizing women's ordination are due to basic ignorance. With reference to the last line, there is only "threefold Buddhism" in my country (Thailand), as the *bhikkhuni* or fully ordained women are missing; hence my prayer.

Strengthening women is to strengthen humankind. Until there is a total understanding of the teachings of Buddha, to include women, we are not the complete "four-fold Buddhism."

LIZ BUDD ELLMANN, MDiv

Liz Budd Ellmann is executive director of Spiritual Directors International, a multi-faith learning community that encourages peace and justice through compassionate, sacred listening (www.sdiworld.org). She previously founded SoulTenders, an organization that taught and supported spiritual practices in the workplace, and served in the Executive Leadership Program at the Jesuit Seattle University. For twenty years, Spiritual Directors International has been helping people around the world and across traditions reclaim the ancient holy art of spiritual companionship. Liz receives great joy from watching birds, walking among big trees, and listening to God bubble up in the stories of people's lives.

Do not try to save
the whole world
or do anything grandiose.
Instead, create
a clearing
in the dense forest
of your life
and wait there
patiently,
until the song
that is yours alone to sing
falls into your open cupped hands
and you recognize and greet it.
Only then will you know
how to give yourself
to this world,
so worthy of rescue.

—Martha Postlethwaite

I recently shared this poem at a multi-faith gathering. Using this poem as a prayer encouraged us to open a clearing for our work together. As servant leaders, when we choose poems and prayers that open space for dialogue at a deep soul level, we help our communities share what we have in common. We discover bridges we might build together toward peace and mutual respect. That might sound grandiose. Yet what I appreciate in the poem is the insistence that clearing a space and patiently waiting for "the song that is yours alone to sing" involves a personal choice that leads to service through a different route.

With so many external demands for our attention—war, famine, drought—choosing to tend our souls may seem small, narcissistic, and risky: "What if it takes a long time?" "What if I can't sing?" "What if I don't know how to tend my soul?" The poem offers hope. Start anywhere. Trust the clearing. Pray. Meditate. Join a spiritual community. Meet regularly with a spiritual director. Read sacred texts and poetry. These are a few ways to create a clearing.

Mysteriously and powerfully, when we nourish the spiritual aspect of our lives, our unique song arrives. We are given inspiration and the courage to sing, to serve, and to build bridges of peace and mutual respect, filled with gratefulness and joy.

FR. LAURENCE FREEMAN, OSB

Laurence Freeman is a Benedictine monk and director of the World Community for Christian Meditation (WCCM). He helped John Main, OSB, establish the first Christian Meditation Centre in London in the 1970s. After John Main died in 1982, Laurence continued his teacher's work in developing a global community. In 1991 he returned to England to establish the International Centre of the WCCM, which is now present in 118 countries (www.wccm.org). Author of many books, Laurence has conducted interreligious dialogues and peace initiatives with the Dalai Lama and other faith leaders. In 2009, he was awarded the Order of Canada for his work.

> Heavenly Father, open our hearts to the silent presence of the spirit of your Son. Lead us into that mysterious silence where your love is revealed to all who call—Maranatha. Come Lord Jesus.
>
> —John Main, OSB

John Main composed this prayer in 1976 for his first set of tapes, shortly after he had begun his public teaching on meditation. It has become the opening prayer for Christian Meditation groups around the world. It expresses both the essence of the Christian understanding of prayer and the sense that we do not pray in isolation but also as members of the community of the Body of Christ.

PROFESSOR MAUREENA FRITZ, PhD, NDS

Maureena Fritz is a Sister of Our Lady of Sion (NDS) and a professor emerita of the Faculty of Theology, University of Toronto, Canada. She is founder of the Bat Kol Institute in Jerusalem (www.batkol.info) whose mission is for "Christians to study the bible within its Jewish milieu, using Jewish sources." She lives in Israel and teaches at the Bat Kol Institute as well as internationally. Author of four books on praying with the Hebrew Scriptures, her most recent book is Daughter of a Voice: I-Thou Encounters in the Book of Genesis. *Maureena received the 2010 Faith and Culture Gold Medal Award from Assumption University, Canada.*

> Hear, O Israel: The LORD is our God, the LORD is one. You shall love the LORD your God with all your heart, and with all your soul, and with all your might. Keep these words that I am commanding you today in your heart. Recite them to your children and talk about them when you are at home and when you are away, when you lie down and when you rise. Bind them as a sign on your hand, fix them as an emblem on your forehead, and write them on the doorposts of your house and on your gates.
>
> —Deuteronomy 6:4–9

These words are known as the *Shema*, "Hear!" Every religious Jew recites these words night and morning. Jesus the Jew recited them every night and morning. In imitation of him, I too recite them night and morning. The words reveal that we can actually love God with strong emotions, that of a lover for the beloved (Song of Songs).

The words also express a motto of behavior: "We will hear and we will do"; in Hebrew, *Sham'nu vey Asinu* (Dt 5:24, The Fox Jewish Translation; Dt 5:27, King James Version). God speaks to us in all the events of our lives. As Martin Buber wrote, "One should beware altogether of understanding the conversation with God . . . as something that occurs merely apart from or above the everyday. God's address to [us] penetrates the events in all our lives and all the events in the world around us . . ." To follow this Voice, we need but take the next right step, and then the next right and we will discover that we have walked a road we never dreamed of walking but one that expresses our authentic self.

DR. RUBINA GILLANI

Dr. Rubina Gillani lives and works in Pakistan where, despite the male-dominated society, she is a successful medical doctor. In the past, she has served as an advisor to the government on public health matters as well as on social welfare and women. Currently, she is country manager for the Fred Hollows Foundation, an international development organization that focuses on blindness prevention and Australian indigenous health (www.hollows.org).

> Worship God; join nothing with Him. Be good to your parents, to relatives, to orphans, to the needy, to neighbors near and far, to travellers in need, and to your slaves. God does not like arrogant, boastful people.
>
> —Qur'an 4:36

I believe this very powerful command for Muslims to carry out *Huqooq ul Ibad* (Our duties toward other human beings) creates the basis for a very strong society and world. Although the main command in Islam refers to our duties to God, I also believe there are important religious responsibilities toward our fellow human beings and these are often ignored by some Muslims.

Allah says we have specific duties toward other people and these are detailed in the Qur'an. They include instructions about our relationships to parents, spouses, children, orphans, neighbors, fellow Muslims, and other people.

I believe that if Muslims, and all humanity, fulfilled *Huqooq ul Ibad* in its true spirit, we could prevent society from fragmenting; for example there would be no need to put parents in nursing homes, no abuse toward vulnerable people such as the disabled, disadvantaged children, orphans, and the poor. Such acts of kindness and compassion toward other people would strengthen the bonds between individuals and strengthen society. They would ultimately spread love and unity among people of all religions and races.

Although I am not particularly religious in the traditional way, the teachings of my religion, Islam, significantly affect my practical life. For me, all religions prescribe similar values of decency and integrity, and without these the good that we see in the world would not be there. However, how religions are followed or interpreted is a different story and is the cause of many miseries.

FETHULLAH GÜLEN

Fethullah Gülen is a Muslim scholar, intellectual, poet, and mystic. Born in Turkey in 1941, he was educated in classical Islamic disciplines and influenced by Said Nursi's teachings. In 1966, he moved to Izmir and began preaching to young Turks, inspiring an "educational and spiritual movement." He moved to the United States in 1999. His support for interfaith dialogue with Jews and Christians has resulted in the establishment of interfaith centers in both Europe and the United States. The organization has evolved into a transnational social movement that runs schools, hospitals, charities, media, and economic institutions. He is author of over sixty books (www.fethullahgulen.org).

O the Exalted One, Whose existence is the life of our lives and Whose divine light is the light of our eyes! You bestowed on us life twice, first by creating us from soil and then by granting us faith and knowledge about You.

Our hearts settled with contentment through attaining knowledge about You. We utter You in our prayers and then hold our breath and wait for the answer that You are going to give. Until this day there has been no one other than You who has heard us, looked upon us, and stroked our heads with mercy. Whatever we found and saw, we owe it to our faith in You, which saved us from astonishment, fear, loneliness, and desolation. O God, from You we wait for perseverance in everything we do, determination

on the pathway of the Qur'an, and sensitivity
toward Your blessings.

—Fethullah Gülen

Prayer is a call, an appeal. It is also a pouring out of the heart from the small to the great, from those on earth to beyond the heavens. It is right to turn toward God with humility, conscious of our servanthood, and to appeal to Him with the language of our weakness, poverty, and neediness. With our prayers, we show our trust in Him and admit that His Power is sufficient for everything; sometimes we can show this by our silence, which, according to some, is more persuasive than the most eloquent speech. Our Lord who is closer to us than we are, says "Pray to me and I will always answer." (Qur'an 40:60).

When a person is able to turn to God wholeheartedly and plead when praying, it means that, as an expression of his trust, he tightly embraces God's eternal power, and with this certainty he can walk toward things that appear to be impossible. "Remember your Lord within yourself most humbly and in awe . . ." (Qur'an 7:205) emphasizes that man should not be distant from his Lord and that, despite God's Majesty, the doors of Mercy and Grace are wide open for everyone.

However, it is not correct to assume that all our prayer requests are going to be fulfilled in line with our wishes. He widens matters that we have narrowed. While enlightening our present, He does not darken our tomorrows. We can overcome anything thanks to His Love, Compassion, and Will.

KIRSTY SWORD GUSMÃO

From 1992 to 1996 Australian-born Kirsty Sword Gusmão worked as a teacher and human rights campaigner in Indonesia. During this time, when the East Timorese struggle for independence was intensifying, she came into contact with the independence leader, Xanana Gusmão, who was serving a twenty-year sentence in a Jakarta jail. Kirsty and Xanana were married in 2000 and now live in the independent Timor-Leste. Kirsty founded the Alola Foundation in 2001 to help local women and their families (www.alolafoundation.org). She became the country's first lady after Xanana became President of Timor-Leste and she is chair of UNESCO's National Commission. Her autobiography is titled A Woman of Independence.

Close your eyes and you will see clearly,
Cease to listen and you will hear the truth.
Be silent and your heart will sing,
Seek no contact and you will find union.
Be still and you will move forward
On the tide of the spirit.
Be gentle and you will need no strength,
Be patient and you will achieve all things.
Be humble and you will remain entire.
—Taoist Meditation

This Taoist meditation resonates with me every time I read it. I like that it is inspired by ancient Chinese religious beliefs and the reflections of *Tao Te Ching*.

TENZIN GYATSO, HIS HOLINESS THE 14TH DALAI LAMA

His Holiness the 14th Dalai Lama describes himself as a simple Buddhist monk despite being spiritual leader of Tibet and, until May 2011, head of state. At the age of two he was recognized as the reincarnation of the 13th Dalai Lama and, at six, he began his monastic education. He assumed full political power in 1950 after China invaded Tibet in 1949. Following the brutal suppression by Chinese troops of Tibet's national uprising in 1959, His Holiness was forced into exile. Since then he has lived in Dharamsala, northern India, the seat of Central Tibetan Administration. His Holiness has appealed to the United Nations, which between 1959 and 1965 adopted three resolutions on Tibet. In 1989 he was awarded the Nobel Peace Prize (www.dalailama.com).

> For as long as space endures,
> And for as long as living beings remain,
> Until then may I, too, abide
> To dispel the misery of the world.
>
> —Shantideva

I say this prayer daily because it gives me great inspiration and determination.

BRENDA HEATHER-LATU

Brenda Heather-Latu is Samoan. She was born and lived in Wellington, New Zealand, for thirty-five years before returning to Samoa, her heartland and the country of origin of her parents, who migrated to New Zealand in the late 1950s. Brenda, a lawyer by profession, was Samoa's first female attorney general, a post she held for nine years. She is now a partner in a local legal firm and undertakes regional consultancies. She is also currently chair of the Pacific Leadership Foundation Board, which aims to develop and strengthen Pacific leaders.

> ...that Christ may dwell in your hearts through faith; that you, being rooted and grounded in love, may be able to comprehend with all the saints what *is* the width and length and depth and height—to know the love of Christ which passes knowledge; that you may be filled with all the fullness of God.
>
> —Ephesians 3:17–19

The world we live in has become increasingly hostile to people of faith, as the foundation of belief in God is challenged and denied. The Bible passage I have chosen is a sobering reminder of the gift bestowed upon mankind which, by grace, seeks no reward yet asks that, by faith, God's love may become our compass and our focus.

Many of the Pacific Island states are known for their commitment to Christian principles and they play an extraordinary role at the heart of these communities.

Living in love and by faith should offer us all a kinder and hope-filled future in the face of challenges such as climate change, global financial crises, endangered species, armed conflict, and diminishing natural resources.

My solemn aspiration is for all our children to live in a caring, gentler, and love-filled global community that keeps returning to faith-filled touchstones to guide their existence.

DR. OBERY M. HENDRICKS, JR.

Dr. Obery Hendricks is one of America's most innovative commentators on religion, politics, and social policy. A former Wall Street investment executive, Obery is now professor of Biblical Interpretation at New York Theological Seminary and a visiting scholar in Religion and African American Studies at Columbia University. He is also a contributor to the Huffington Post, *an affiliated scholar at the Center for American Progress, and a board member of the Public Religion Research Institute in Washington, DC. His books include* The Universe Bends Toward Justice: Radical Reflections on the Bible, the Church, and the Body Politic *and* The Politics of Jesus: Rediscovering the True Revolutionary Nature of Jesus' Teachings and How They Have Been Corrupted, *which* The Washington Post *called "essential reading for Americans."*

Grant us, O God, the vision and the will to be found on the right side in the great battle for bread, which rages round us, in strike and turmoil and litigation. Let us remember that here as so often elsewhere no impossible wisdom is asked of [humanity], only Thine ancient sacrifice—to do justly and love mercy and walk humbly—to refuse to use, of the world's goods, more than we earn, to be generous with those that earn but little and to avoid the vulgarity that flaunts wealth and clothes and ribbons in the face of poverty. These things are the sins that lie beneath our labor wars, and from such sins defend us, O Lord. Amen.

Give us grace, O God, to dare to do the deed which we well know cries to be done. Let

> us not hesitate because of ease, or the words of [other's] mouths, or our own lives. Mighty causes are calling us—the freeing of women, the training of children, the putting down of hate and murder and poverty—all these and more. But they call with voices that mean work and sacrifice and death. Mercifully grant us, O God, the spirit of Esther, that we say: I will go unto the King and if I perish, I perish. Amen.
>
> —William Edward Burghardt Du Bois

I love these prayers because the plaintive plea of Du Bois reflects what I believe to be the holistic spirituality of Jesus, expressed in his conflation of Deuteronomy 6:5 and Leviticus 19:18 into what he pronounced as the greatest of divine commandments: "You shall love your Lord your God with all your heart, with all your soul and with all your mind . . . And . . . you shall love your neighbor as yourself" (Mt 22:37–39).

In my estimation, Jesus' pronouncement is holistically spiritual because it defines spirituality as having two equally crucial axes, one horizontal ("Love your Lord"), the other vertical ("Love your neighbor"), together constituting the cross, the greatest symbol of self-sacrificial love.

Thus, Jesus' directive to love our neighbors as ourselves is an admonition to honor God in the primary, if not the only way we can: to actively strive to ensure the same well-being and peace of mind for our neighbors and their loved ones that we seek for ourselves and those we call our own. That is what the prayers of Du Bois ask of God: for the strength and the unflagging love to struggle so our every neighbor might have life with abundance in every sphere of life.

THE RIGHT REVEREND RICHARD HOLLOWAY

Richard Holloway was Bishop of Edinburgh and Primus of the Scottish Episcopal Church until 2000. He was Gresham Professor of Divinity in the City of London from 1997 to 2001 and chairman of the Scottish Arts Council from 2005 to 2010. He is a Fellow of the Royal Society of Edinburgh. He is also a broadcaster and author of twenty-eight books, including Looking in the Distance: The Human Search for Meaning *and* How to Read the Bible.

From the place where we are right
flowers will never grow
in the spring.

The place where we are right
is hard and trampled
like a yard.

But doubts and loves
dig up the world
like a mole, a plow.
And a whisper will be heard in the place
where the ruined
house once stood.

—Yehuda Amichai

I interviewed Yehuda Amichai, Israel's most famous poet, not long before he died, at his home in Jerusalem. He was a tolerant, humorous man, without religion himself, but bemused by the violent role it played in the land he loved and the city in which he lived. Indeed, in another of his poems, "Ecology of Jerusalem," he had said that the air of Jerusalem was so saturated with prayers and dreams that it was hard to breathe, as though a cloud of metaphysical smog hung over the holy city.

I think Amichai's poem about the perils of being right points to one of the dangers of religion: our certainties—in a world where so little is certain—can make us haters and persecutors of the certainties of others, something that religion is all too prone to. But in contrast to the certainties that make us hard, Amichai points to the way our doubts and loves can cause all sorts of lovely flowers to bloom, such as tolerance and compassion. It is often forgotten that the opposite of faith is not doubt, but certainty. Faith has to be co-active with doubt or it is not faith, but its opposite, certainty. More faith and less certainty would make the religions of the world more humble and compassionate, something that is devoutly to be wished.

DAISAKU IKEDA

Daisaku Ikeda is a Buddhist leader, peace-builder, prolific writer, poet, educator, and founder of a number of cultural, educational, and peace research institutions. As third president of the Soka Gakkai in Japan and founder of the Soka Gakkai International (SGI), he has inspired a movement numbering more than twelve million people around the world. Based on the seven-hundred-year-old tradition of Nichiren Buddhism, the SGI is characterized by its emphasis on individual empowerment and social engagement to advance peace, culture, and education (www.daisakuikeda.org).

> Cherry, plum, peach, damson—all, just as they are, are entities possessing their own unique qualities.
>
> —Nichiren

Buddhism uses the concept of the cherry, the plum, the peach, and the damson to explain the importance of respecting our diversity. The cherry has its distinct beauty, the plum its delicate fragrance, the peach its lovely color, the damson its special flavor. Likewise, each person has a unique mission, his or her own individuality and way of living.

It is important to recognize and respect this. In the natural world too, meaning lies in diversity. Traditional Japanese culture has described the diversity of human society with the phrase "myriads of flowers blossoming in profusion." The purpose of each human life is to develop one's special individuality—to blossom—to the greatest possible extent. Philosophy refers to this as "self-realization"; in the Buddhism practiced by the SGI, we describe it as "human revolution."

The very fact that we have been born in this world demonstrates we have a mission that only we can fulfill. We would not have been born otherwise. Nothing is meaningless in the universe—everything has some kind of significance. Everyone has his or her own unique personality: that is what makes life interesting. How dull the world would be if we were all the same.

Nevertheless, it is crucial to realize that our true individuality cannot blossom without our making the utmost effort. It would be a big mistake to feel that what we are now is all we can ever hope to become. Change is intrinsic to our humanity. Although everyone is different, we all possess tremendous potential. We can become capable of great deeds if we set our minds to it. What we must never do is to abandon faith in ourselves, to limit our potential by thinking, "this is all I am."

However tough the circumstances we face, we must never lose our belief in ourselves. Comparing oneself with others and developing a sense of inferiority—or of superiority—is a truly wretched way of living. Only when individuals resolve to devote their lives to fulfilling their potential, making constant efforts to achieve this, can their true individuality shine forth. Persons who live in this way will be truly capable of respecting the uniqueness of others and appreciate in their heart the true importance of diversity.

YUSUF ISLAM

Yusuf Islam, formerly known as Cat Stevens, is a globally admired British musician and singer-songwriter. In 1977 he embraced Islam, leaving the music industry and becoming an energetic supporter of educational and philanthropic causes, including founding Muslim Aid and Small Kindness (www.smallkindness.org). His international fame and reputation have made him one of most influential cultural figures within the Muslim world. Since 1995, he has gradually returned to the studio and music making. Yusuf is a vocal opponent of terrorism and extremism and in 2004 was recognized with the Man of Peace award by the Nobel Peace Prize Laureates Committee.

It is not righteousness
That you turn your faces
Towards East or West;
But it is righteousness
To believe in Allah
And the Last Day,
And the Angels,
And the Book,
And the Messengers;
To spend of your substance,
Out of love for Him,
For your kin,
For orphans,
For the needy,
For the wayfarer,
For those who ask,

And for the ransom of slaves;
To be steadfast in prayer,
And practice regular charity;
To fulfill the contracts
Which you have made;
And to be firm and patient,
In pain (or suffering),
And adversity
And throughout
All periods of panic.
Such are the people
Of truth, the God-fearing.

–Qur'an 2:177

One of my favorite passages of the Holy Qur'an sets the standard for true faith and virtue in the sight of God. Away from the externals often focused on by observers of the faith of Islam, this verse puts the heart of the religion—closeness to God and true sincerity to Him—at the core. It is telling us that actions are the profoundest and most effective way of demonstrating we have faith—and demonstrating it not necessarily to others, but to God Himself.

B. K. S. IYENGAR

B. K. S. Iyengar (Guruji) is a world renowned yoga teacher, philanthropist, and philosopher who has been practicing yoga for more than seventy-five years. Born in 1918 in India, he was introduced to yoga at the age of sixteen by the well-known yogi Sri Tirumalai Krishnamacharya. He began teaching yoga in the West in the 1950s as a result of his work with violinist Yehudi Menuhin. In 1975, B. K. S. Iyengar established the Ramamani Iyengar Memorial Yoga Institute in Pune, India, where students are taught the essence of Iyengar yoga. Author of many books including the acclaimed Light on Yoga, *Mr. Iyengar, well into his nineties, continues to teach and practice today (www.bksiyengar.com).*

My body is my temple and bow.
My *sadhana* or practice of *asanas* [yoga postures]
 are my arrows (or prayers)
My target is the Self or Purusa.

—B. K. S. Iyengar

I am a devotee of yoga and the above prayer explains my way of life. When I practice I am a philosopher, when I teach I am a scientist, and when I demonstrate I am an artist.

As I wrote in *Light on Yoga*, "It is by the coordinated and concentrated efforts of his body, senses, mind, reason and Self that a man obtains the prize of inner peace and fulfills the quest of his soul to meet his Maker. The supreme adventure in a man's life is his journey back to his Creator."

DADI JANKI

Dadi Janki is administrative head of the Brahma Kumaris World Spiritual University, a worldwide network of organizations with members from all walks of life who acknowledge the intrinsic goodness of all people (www.bkwsu.org). Dadi moved from India to London in 1974 to oversee the organization's teachings spread to more than 130 countries. She returned to India in 2007. Internationally acknowledged as a spiritual leader, Dadi's lifelong focus has been to align her mind and heart to God's will and purpose.

I used to say, "I am a Hindu,
You are a Christian"
I could never say that anymore
My attitude has changed
Now I would say
"Whether you are standing before a statue of Christ
or worshiping the image of Krishna
God is still the one Father and–
We are all the children of the one Father"
Religion no longer exists in the world
in a true form
When merely ritualistic
it is superficial and without power
Where there is real understanding
where there is truth in words
there is also power
Power would not be received from God
in order for us to fight each other

Power is received
for us to become Peaceful
True religion says, "Peace"
True religion teaches Peace
—Dadi Janki

These words resonate with the truth within my being. They remind me who I am, who I belong to, and what it is I have to do. I also value the Brahma Kumaris expression: *Om shanti—I, the soul, am a being of peace.*

Brahma Kumaris World Spiritual University teaches a practical method of meditation that helps individuals understand their inner strengths and values. Raja Yoga Meditation is a method of relaxing, refreshing, and clearing the mind and heart. It helps you look inside to rediscover and reconnect with your original spiritual essence. Meditation enables an integration of your spiritual identity with the social and physical realities around you, restoring a functional and healthy balance between your inner and outer worlds.

MONICA JEDDAH OTTO

Monica Otto was born in Budbi, a remote village in East Sepik Province, Papua New Guinea. Educated in a Catholic mission school, she gained tertiary degrees from Natural Resource and Environment University and Queensland University of Technology. Monica runs the Foundation of Women In Agriculture Development (FOWIAD), a non-governmental organization that provides services to marginalized women and their families in remote indigenous communities. FOWIAD also provides employment opportunities for female agricultural graduates. After an unfulfilling career in government, Monica's dream to create a process for community capacity development is now a reality.

Early in my career I was asked in a management course to name a leader I admired. I wrote "Jesus Christ" on the board. Although the other participants were bemused by my choice, as it did not fit their perceptions, I made no apology for my choice.

Jesus showed us He was faithful and obedient to the will of His Father, Jehovah. His message was one of love, the love of the other. If I obey His commandments, He values me. As Jesus said, "My Father and I will live in you and you in Me," [paraphrase of John 14:11, 23]. This is the most powerful, profound divine union, and my strength.

If no one understands me, I can always retreat into His presence where I find Him by playing with children, working in a garden, or

> talking to abused women and holding their afflicted children in my arms. Laughter and joy become spontaneous as we value our friendship and trust in Jesus Christ.
>
> I fear the Lord our God for He is TRUTH; this fear has made me embrace all living and non-living things as belonging to Truth. My work is obedience to Him through the poor and the needy. If our life's destiny is centered only on our five senses, then it is earthly, but if we can connect from within and find an internal spirit of Truth, it becomes heavenly. This is pure love that has no boundaries. This is the love that Jesus talks about.
>
> —Monica Jeddah Otto

I continue to obtain great inspiration from the Bible. I tried to memorize many passages, but my ability to quote Bible verses did not satisfy my desire to please my Jehovah. It was not until I realized that the word of God lived in me and I expressed His word through my actions that I felt the real presence of Jesus in my life. The scriptures give me confirmation of the validity of my actions.

My achievements have also come with a great sacrifice. Those who have suffered are those who are dear to me. My work has separated me from my family. Having a very supportive husband together with my five adult children is the foundation of my success. My officers have stood by me as I struggled to generate an income for them. My organization members have supported and believed in me. It is all these whom I wish to acknowledge. And even to those who are jealous of my efforts and try to undo our achievements, their negativity only enhances my resolve to succeed.

SHAYKH MUHAMMAD HISHAM KABBANI

Shaykh Muhammad Hisham Kabbani is one of the world's leading scholars of Islamic history and the spiritual science of Sufism. As deputy leader of the Naqshbandi Haqqani Sufi Order, Shaykh Kabbani also serves as a guide and teacher to approximately two million Muslims in the United States, the United Kingdom, Southeast Asia, Australia, and other countries throughout the world. He is chair and founder of the Islamic Supreme Council of America and is dedicated to spreading the key teachings of Islam—peace, tolerance, respect, and love—throughout the world. He is an outspoken critic of extremism.

In the Name of God, The Compassionate, The Merciful. All Praise is for God, the Lord of all creations, and praise and peace upon His prophets and messengers and upon His Prophet Muhammad and his pure family and his noble companions and on all those who follow their guidance until the Final Hour.

Oh our Lord, make the beginning of this day goodness, and its middle happiness, and its end success. Oh our Lord, make its beginning mercy, its middle bounty and its ending generosity and forgiveness. All praise be to God who humbled everything before His Greatness, made all things subservient before His Honor, brought low all things before His Kingship and made all things submit to His power. And all praise to God who made all things tranquil before His Majesty, and made everything appear through His wisdom,

> and humbled all things before His Pride. Oh our
> Lord, cause us to awaken in the time most
> beloved to Yourself, O Loving One.
>
> —Mawlana Shaykh Nazim Adil Al-Haqqani

I chose this prayer because it exemplifies the Islamic concept that says we are to ask our Lord for goodness in both this life and in the next. It reminds me of the teachings of Sayyedina Ali, the nephew and companion of the Prophet Mohammed, who taught us to do in this life as if we are going to live forever and to do for the next life as if we will die today.

This prayer also reminds me of the majesty of our Lord's dominion over creation and how much we need His grace and mercy, every minute of every day.

DR. INDERJIT KAUR

Dr. Inderjit Kaur is a medical doctor and patron President of Pingalwara Society (www.pingalwaraonline.org). Bhagat Puran Singh, the founder of Pingalwara Society, nominated Dr. Kaur as his successor before he died in 1992. She has continued his work in serving humanity in a similar selfless way by helping the destitute and orphans, the mentally handicapped and those suffering terminal and incurable diseases. Recipient of many national and international awards, Dr. Kaur was awarded the Padma Bhushan Award from the Indian Government in 2008, for her distinguished service to the nation.

> O Lord, Give me Thy blessings that I may not be deterred from meritorious deeds, that I may not be afraid of the adversary, when I go out to fight and that I may win through faith, my inner conscience remaining as my guide. I crave that I may ever sing Thy praises and when the last moment comes, I may fall fighting heroically in the battlefield.
>
> —Sri Guru Gobind Singh Ji

In Sikhism, Sri Guru Gobind Singh Ji offered this prayer to the Almighty which has become the inspiring prayer of his followers.

The aim of writing this piece was to inspire the common man to rise up against the tyrannical rulers of the time and to fight and sacrifice all they had for their freedom. It invokes the blessings of the Almighty God.

The collection of writings attributed to Sri Guru Gobind Singh Ji is known as the Dasam Granth. It is a compilation of hymns, philosophical writings, an autobiography of the Guru and many fables. The underlying message of all the works is "worship the creator and not the creations."

BRUCE KENT

Bruce Kent was educated in Canada and England. He served in the British Army between 1947-1949, was ordained a priest in 1958 and retired in 1987. His peace and justice initiatives include general secretary and chairperson of the Campaign for Nuclear Disarmament (CND), 1980-90, chair of War on Want, president of the International Peace Bureau, and founding chair of Movement for the Abolition of War which aims to convince people that wars are not inevitable (www.abolishwar.org.uk). Currently he is vice-president of CND, Pax Christi UK, and chair of Progressing Prisoners Maintaining Innocence which supports high risk prisoners whose assertions of innocence hinder their release.

> Even if I write these words with my hands in chains, I still find that much better than if my will were in chains. Neither prison, nor chains, nor sentence of death, can separate me from the love of God, can rob a man of his faith and his free will. Obviously, God gives so much strength to those who love Him and who do not give priority to the world rather than to eternity. The power of God cannot be overcome.
>
> —Franz Jägerstätter

Few people have had such a profound influence on my life as Franz Jägerstätter. Having served in the British Armed Forces, it is Jägerstätter's message to the world's military that is most significant to me. Despite efforts by those who want to put him in a safe category, there is no evidence that Franz was an absolute pacifist. A military reservist since his short period of military training in 1940, he was patriotic and there is no reason to suppose that he would have been unwilling to defend his country had it been attacked.

One of the few in his village (St. Radegund) to openly oppose the takeover of Austria by Hitler's Germany, his resistance to the new regime grew in the subsequent years and eventually became a matter of official comment. When called up again in 1943, Jägerstätter, a pious and even rigid Catholic, refused to take the unconditional oath of obedience to the Führer and he said he would take no part in a war which he believed to be quite unjust.

The courage of Franz Jägerstätter obliges us all to find other ways of resolving our conflicts. It is my belief that wars today are bound to be unjust. Nonviolent solutions to conflict are available. The death and destruction that wars cause are beyond any possible proportion.

Since 1975, many pilgrims make their way annually to St. Radegund on August 9, the anniversary of Jägerstätter's death, and come away inspired and renewed in their own commitment to peacemaking. I feel that the courage and conviction that allows a man to write such words hours before his execution is breathtaking.

SIMON KEYES

Simon Keyes comes from a family of Church of England parish priests. After he graduated with a degree in zoology, his career changed to cultivating new initiatives in homelessness, mental health and crime prevention. Later he worked for the World Community for Christian Meditation, and organized The Way of Peace, an interfaith initiative in Northern Ireland with the Dalai Lama. Currently, Simon is Director of St. Ethelburga's Centre for Reconciliation and Peace in London which aims to promote understanding of the relationship between faith and conflict (www.stethelburgas.org). A keen walker, Simon is writing a book about walking alone from Budapest to London.

God of life

Every act of violence,
Between myself and others
    Destroys a part of your creation

Stir in my heart
A renewed sense of reverence
    For all life

Give me vision to recognize your spirit
In every human being,
    However they behave towards me

Make possible the impossible
By cultivating in me
    The fertile seed of healing love

May I play my part
In breaking the cycle of violence
By realizing that
Peace begins with me.

The team at St. Ethelburga's wrote this prayer on July 7, 2005, the day four young Muslim men killed fifty-two people with bombs in London.

AZIM KHAMISA

Azim Khamisa founded the Tariq Khamisa Foundation (www.tkf.org) to honor his twenty year old son, Tariq, who was senselessly murdered by Tony Hicks, a fourteen year old gang member. The Foundation is committed to halting the continuing cycle of youth violence through delivering programs on peace and non-violence to schools and corporations. His grief has now been transformed into forgiveness. He often co-presents with Tony's grandfather, Ples Felix. Author of four books, Azim is recipient of many awards including Building Peaceful Communities Award and has spoken alongside the Dalai Lama in the Synthesis Dialogues in 2004.

It takes sustained goodwill to create friendship...
It takes sustained friendship to create trust
It takes sustained trust to create empathy
It takes sustained empathy to create compassion
It takes sustained compassion to create peace.
But people ask me all the time–
    how do you extend goodwill
    to the person who murdered your son?

I tell them you do it through forgiveness.

As it is evident it worked for me and my family.
What is a miracle it worked for him and his family.

It can work for you and your family.

It can work for Israel and Palestine
It can work for North and South Korea
It can work for Afghanistan, Iran, Iraq and the USA

Indeed it can work for the planet.

My sisters and brothers I believe Peace is possible.
How do I know that?

Because I am at peace.

—Azim Khamisa

This quote is the basis of my fourth book *From Fulfillment to Peace*. The quote was also inspired by the "9/11" tragedy and my relationship with the grandfather and guardian of my son's killer, Ples Felix. I call this quote "my peace formula."

DAISY KHAN

Daisy Khan is executive director of the American Society for Muslim Advancement (ASMA), a New York-based non-profit organization dedicated to strengthening an expression of Islam based on cultural and religious harmony. At ASMA, she has launched two groundbreaking flagship programs: Muslim Leaders of Tomorrow (MLT), a global network of one thousand civil society leaders, and Women's Islamic Initiative in Spirituality and Equality (WISE), a global movement to empower Muslim women (www.wisemuslimwomen.org).

> Indeed Allah (God) will not change the conditions of a community (or a people) until they change what is in themselves.
>
> –Qur'an 13:11

This verse from the Qur'an resonates with me spiritually on both a personal and societal level. On a personal level, it reminds me of the importance of self-reflection and self-examination in my own life. Often through the hectic routine of daily life we forget to take a moment to examine if our actions conform to the qualities that are so central to our personal individuality. It is religion that helps us in this quest for individual betterment, pushing us to strive for perfection. Islam says that it is God who leads us through inner change, giving us the capacity to achieve the highest levels among all of God's creation. As Qur'an 95:4 states, "We create man in the finest state."

Jelal al-Din Rumi, a thirteenth-century mystic and poet, believed that the perfected human being (*insan-i kamil*) stood even above angels in the order of creation. Self-reflection and self-examination are the first steps on the path towards perfection and will always be needed to make progress on this journey.

This principle, however, extends beyond the individual and calls all to improve their community and society at large. My own journey for self-improvement led me to examine the conditions of Muslim women throughout the world and act as the catalyst for all of the advocacy work that I undertake. My passion for grassroots social justice movements is rooted in my conviction that we are all called to better our world. Distorted understandings of our religion have been used to justify a series of transgressions against women and children. The Qur'an reminds us that it is up to us, as imperfect beings, to drive change from within.

SHAYKHA HALIMA KRAUSEN

Born into a German Protestant/Catholic family, Halima found her own way to Islam in her early teens. She studied Islamic law and theology and is currently Imam of the German-speaking Muslim Community in Hamburg. She helped found the educational institute Initiative of Islamic Studies and was part of a team that translated the Qur'an into German. She is a teacher and a frequent speaker at conferences in Germany, the United Kingdom, the United States, and the Middle East, especially in the context of interfaith dialogue. Her books include a collection of her sermons and an anthology of prayers from the Islamic tradition (www.halimakrausen.com).

In the name of God, the Beneficent, the Merciful.
Praise is due to God, the Creator and Sustainer
 of the worlds,
the Beneficent, the Merciful, the Master of the
 Day of Judgment.
It is You whom we serve, and it is You whom we
 ask for help.
Guide us on the straight path,
the path of those on whom You bestow grace,
not of those who incur anger nor of those who
 go astray.

–Qur'an 1:1–7

This Surah (chapter) is the most central prayer in Islam. But what makes it special for me is its request for guidance. The world that I grew up in and that I now live and work in is very complex. I enjoy its colorful diversity of languages, cultures, religions, and spiritual paths. The Qur'an speaks to my heart when it points out the differences in minerals, plants, animals, and humans as signs of the One Creator.

At the same time, I am painfully aware of the bitter misunderstandings and conflicts that cause destruction, suffering, and death, and of the difficulties of navigating a world where solutions are far from simple. Orientation is provided in our sacred scriptures and traditions, but we also need help in everyday decisions and in our constant struggle both with our own impulses and inclinations and with the hostility of others. I therefore pray for guidance as a way of peace and understanding in creation, in society, and with the Creator—not just for myself, but for all those involved in important decision-making and for all humankind.

DR. SUNITHA KRISHNAN

Indian-born Dr. Sunitha Krishnan is a widely celebrated activist against human trafficking. Since receiving her PhD in social work Sunitha has devoted her life to this cause. As co-founder and general secretary of Prajwala (eternal flame), Sunitha has rescued thousands of women and children from commercial sexual exploitation and worked to restore their dignity. In collaboration with government departments and non-governmental organizations, she has established schools and provided jobs to rehabilitate many of the girls and women (www.prajwalaindia.com). Her awards include the Perdita Huston Human Rights Award, the CNN Real Hero award, and the Stree Shakti Puraskar (Woman Power Award) from the Indian government.

> Primal Shakti, I bow to thee
> All-encompassing Shakti, I bow to thee
> That through which God creates, I bow to thee
> Creative power of the Kundalini (dormant energy)
> Mother of all, to thee I bow.
>
> —Kautilya Chanakaya

This is a mantra taken from the Vedas; it is a popular chant by the early Indian writer Chanakaya. It strikes a deep chord in me as I strive to bring out the inherent *shakti* (power) in women to fight against the many adversities they face in their daily lives.

It calls upon the Divine-Mother Power and her primal protective energy. Any rejoicing in the female power is a great source of strength for me. Chanting it gives me an immense sense of energy as it both celebrates and salutes the power and resilience of a woman.

THE REVEREND UNA KROLL

Una Kroll has had a long journey in her Christian life as a woman, wife, mother of four, doctor of medicine, Anglican priest, ecumenist, author of Christian books, and a peace and justice worker. She now lives a "life of prayer" in retirement and is not engaged in any active ministry outside her home.

> . . . I will call you brother, even though you will
> not call me sister.
> I will reach out to you, even though you will not
> reach out to me,
> I will affirm our mutuality as persons seeking to
> make a common witness,
> even though you are not free to do so.
> —Peggy Ann Way

I was made a deaconess in the Church of England in 1970, and in that same year I founded the Christian Parity Group, a collective of men and women who wanted to support people all over the world, people who had been denied some human rights solely because they were women.

At the same time, we decided to challenge the institutional sexism of some Christian churches that denied that women could be representatives of Christ as ordained ministers of their churches. I was then, and still am, a peace and justice worker, committed to nonviolence. So when I came across Peggy Ann Way's prayer, I adopted it as a Christian way of resistance to the manifest injustices that I and others suffered at the hands of the Church and State. In one of my early books for women, I wrote, "These words have burnt themselves into my life as a kind of prayer that I use to remind myself of the humanity of those who are sexists." As the struggle has continued in succeeding years, it has expanded to include all those who are oppressed through their gender identity.

In recent years I have modified the prayer and replaced "will not" with "cannot" in each phrase of the prayer because during these past fifty years Christ has clothed me with mercy and compassion. He has increased my love for all oppressors, and oppressive institutions, whom I now see to be oppressed by their inability to liberate those over whom they have power. But I still say this prayer every day of my life.

PROFESSOR DR. HANS KÜNG

One of the world's best known living theologians, Professor Küng was born in Switzerland, ordained a Catholic priest in 1954, and taught at Tübingen University. His writings became controversial when he questioned doctrines such as papal infallibility, and in 1979 the Vatican banned him from teaching. He was later allowed to teach under secular rather than Catholic auspices. Professor Küng has written more than forty books including On Being a Christian, Judaism, *and* Global Responsibility, *and he was a catalyst in founding the Global Ethic Foundation of which he is President (www.weltethos.de). His many awards include one from the Temple of Understanding for "extraordinary service to interreligious understanding."*

Hidden, eternal, immeasurable God, rich in
mercy,
there is no other God than you.
You are great and worthy of all praise.
Your power and grace sustain the universe.
God of truth without falsity, righteous and true,
you chose Abraham your submissive servant
to be the father of many peoples
and spoke through the prophets.
Hallowed and praised be your name in all the
world,
and let your will be done wherever people live.
Living and gracious God, hear our prayer:
our guilt has become great.
Forgive us children of Abraham our wars,
our enmities, our misdeeds against one another.

Redeem us from all distress and give us peace.
Guide of our destiny,
bless the leaders and rulers of the states,
that they do not lust after power and glory
but act responsibly for the well-being of their
    subjects
and peace among all.
Guide our religious communities and their
    leaders,
so that they not only proclaim the message of
    peace
but live it out themselves.
And to all of us, and those who are not of us,
give your grace, mercy and all good things,
and lead us, God of the living,
on the right way to your eternal glory.

—Hans Küng

A certain consensus is developing among Christians and I believe this interreligious prayer is an expression of the coming together of all the "scattered children of God" and could be prayed together by Jews, Christians, and Muslims.

PROFESSOR CHUNG HYUN KYUNG

Born in Korea, Chung Hyun Kyung is professor of ecumenical theology at Union Theological Seminary in New York City. She is also an author, a Christian eco-feminist theologian, and a Buddhist dharma teacher in the Korean Zen tradition. At the World Council of Churches 1991 Canberra Conference, her interpretation of a feminist Asian, Third World "Holy Spirit" caused a sensation. In 1999, she lived for a year as a Buddhist novice nun in the Himalayas. Recently she completed a pilgrimage to eighteen Muslim countries to dialogue with Muslim women peacemakers. She is now writing a book on her encounters with them.

Don't wish for perfect health. In perfect health there is greed and wanting. So an ancient said, "Make good medicine from the suffering of sickness."

Don't hope for a life without problems. An easy life results in a judgmental and lazy mind. So an ancient once said, "Accept the anxieties and difficulties of this life."

Don't expect your practice to be always clear of obstacles. Without hindrances the mind that seeks enlightenment may be burnt out. So an ancient once said, "Attain deliverance in disturbances"...

Make friends but don't expect any benefit for yourself. Friendship only for oneself harms trust. So an ancient once said, "Have an enduring friendship with purity in heart."

Don't expect others to follow your direction. When it happens that others go along with you, it results in pride. So an ancient once said, "Use your will to bring peace between people."

Expect no reward for an act of charity. Expecting something in return leads to a scheming mind. So an ancient once said, "Throw false spirituality away like a pair of old shoes"...

Be equal to every hindrance. Buddha attained Supreme Enlightenment without hindrance. Seekers after truth are schooled in adversity. When they are confronted by a hindrance, they can't be overcome. Then, cutting free, their treasure is great.

—Kyong Ho

This is a popular prayer among Korean Buddhist practitioners. Whenever I feel life is not what I want, but what it is and what makes me suffer, I read this prayer to try and make my heart calm and peaceful.

Korean Zen Master Seung Sahn answered a young seeker who asked him "What is Buddhism?" by replying "Buddhism is ENOUGH mind"! Appreciation and acceptance of "what it is" is the "ENOUGH mind" from which every transformation and happiness become possible. This is not a passive resignation, rather a radical acceptance. Become like the water, flow like the stream and you will understand harmony. This is the "Water's Way" of finding peace, happiness, and quiet courage to change what needs to be changed.

This prayer teaches us to "melt and flow" to the ocean of enlightenment even if our existence feels like solid frozen ice. You do not try to change other people or your circumstances first. You must try to change yourself by "melting" your karma and solid ego first. Then everything changes. This is the "Water's Way" of liberation.

DR. JOANNA MACY

Joanna Macy, PhD, is an eco-philosopher and scholar of Buddhism, systems theory, and deep ecology. A prominent activist, Joanna has created a groundbreaking theoretical framework for personal and social change, as well as a powerful workshop methodology for its application. Joanna's many workshops address the psychological and spiritual issues of the nuclear age, the cultivation of ecological awareness, and the fruitful resonance between Buddhist thought and contemporary science. The auhor of many books, including Coming Back to Life: Practices to Reconnect Our Lives *and her memoir* Widening Circles, *Joanna lives in California (www.joannamacy.net).*

Quiet friend who has come so far,
feel how your breathing makes more space
    around you.
Let this darkness be a bell tower
and you the bell. As you ring,

what batters you becomes your strength.
Move back and forth into the change.
What is it like, such intensity of pain?
If the drink is bitter, turn yourself to wine.

In this uncontainable night,
be the mystery at the crossroads of your senses,
the meaning discovered there.

And if the world has ceased to hear you,
say to the silent Earth: I flow.
To the rushing water, speak: I am.

—Rainer Maria Rilke (*Sonnets to Orpheus*, II, 29)

I worked on this sonnet from Rilke's *Sonnets to Orpheus* with my co-translator, Anita Barrows, during the United States invasion of Iraq in 2003. In that spiritually bleak time, the poet's words and images heartened me greatly. They reconnected me to deeper sources of strength and courage.

MAIREAD CORRIGAN MAGUIRE

Mairead Corrigan Maguire became active with the peace movement in Northern Ireland in 1976 when her sister's three children were killed by a getaway car after the driver was fatally shot by a soldier. Over 100,000 people were involved in the initial protest movement, Community of Peace People, founded by Mairead, Betty Williams, and Ciaran McKeown. Mairead and Betty were awarded the 1976 Nobel Peace Prize in recognition of their work for peace. With the organization now called Peace People (www.peacepeople.com), Mairead continues to engage in dialogue and peace initiatives in many countries including Palestine and Israel. In 2006, Mairead co-founded the Nobel Women's Initiative, which aims to strengthen women's rights around the world.

O Lord, make me an instrument of thy peace!
Where there is hatred, let me sow love.
Where there is injury, pardon.
where there is discord, harmony.
where there is doubt, faith.
where there is despair, hope.
where there is darkness, light.
where there is sorrow, joy.

Oh Divine Master, grant that I may not so much
seek
to be consoled as to console;
to be understood as to understand;
to be loved as to love;

for it is in giving that we receive;
it is in pardoning that we are pardoned;
and it is in dying that we are born to eternal life.

—Attributed to St. Francis of Assisi

I have always loved this prayer. My husband Jack and I have a love of St. Francis and St. Clare, and after we were married in Rome, we went to Assisi on our honeymoon! Clare (a woman of prayer) and Francis (a man of prayer and action) speak to us as models of those with compassionate hearts. They were people who were before their time in connecting spirituality and politics and environment and love of all life and creation.

NELSON MANDELA

Nelson Mandela is an international statesman and visionary. He led the fight against apartheid in South Africa as head of the African National Congress's armed wing and served twenty-seven years in prison. When freed in 1990, he supported reconciliation and helped lead South Africa's transition to a multi-racial democracy. His call for forgiveness for his former white oppressors inspired the whole world. In 1994, he became the first president of a democratic South Africa. He has received many awards, including, in 1993, the Nobel Peace Prize. In November 2009, the United Nations General Assembly declared July 18 "Nelson Mandela International Day" to mark his contribution to peace. The Nelson Mandela Foundation "embodies the spirit of reconciliation, ubuntu, *and social justice" (www.nelsonmandela.org).*

Out of the night that covers me,
Black as the Pit from pole to pole,
I thank whatever gods may be
For my unconquerable soul.

In the fell clutch of circumstance
I have not winced nor cried aloud.
Under the bludgeonings of chance
My head is bloody, but unbowed.

Beyond this place of wrath and tears
Looms but the Horror of the shade,
And yet the menace of the years
Finds, and shall find, me unafraid.

It matters not how strait the gate,
How charged with punishments the scroll.
I am the master of my fate:
I am the captain of my soul.

—William Earnest Henley

When you read works of that nature you become encouraged. It puts life in you. (Nelson Mandela 1993).

KATHERINE MARSHALL

Katherine Marshall has worked for over three decades on international development, with a focus on issues facing the world's poorest countries. She is a senior fellow at Georgetown's Berkley Center for Religion, Peace and World Affairs, a senior advisor at the World Bank, and executive director of the World Faiths Development Dialogue. Katherine has written several books and also writes a blog called "Faith in Action" for the Newsweek/Washington Post *website "On Faith." Information on her current work on bridging development and faith can be found on the Berkley Center website (http://berkleycenter. georgetown.edu/programs/religion-and-global-development).*

With the drawing of this Love and
the voice of this Calling

We shall not cease from exploration
And the end of all our exploring
Will be to arrive where we started
And know the place for the first time.

—T. S. Eliot

Love, the adventure of learning, and the perpetual search for understanding together are the essence of the human challenge. Love, learning, and understanding can come only with a ceaseless examination of the world around us. And that challenge calls for a constant reflection on what I, as an individual, can contribute, what makes up that voice of calling.

Eliot's poetry has always been an inspiration. Every reading suggests new nuances and helps toward a deeper understanding. It also prompts new questions. This passage not only highlights the beauty of intellectual adventure, but also the balance between external exploration and learning from different places, disciplines, and people, grounded in roots, history, family, and those close to hand. It is about dreams and practical daily life.

In the fight against global poverty and for a more just and creative world, knowledge, dialogue, and true engagement of different experiences and perspectives are the keys. We learn all the time, and in doing so hone our understanding of both challenges and solutions. Ethical partnership, empowerment, and equity are tough but deeply meaningful goals at the heart of the effort to work for a better and fairer world. Yet each goal is understood differently by different people in different times and places. There are many players in a turning kaleidoscope. Returning to each concept and challenge with the insight of exploration, they seem richer and still more vital. And the path to translating ideals into practice is clearer and more inspirational.

DR. WANJIKU MATHENGE

The eldest of six children, Wanjiku was told by her father that her education would be her only inheritance. She represented Kenya in tennis at the All Africa Games but decided to become a doctor and, later, an ophthalmologist. Currently, as the Eastern Africa medical advisor for the Fred Hollows Foundation, she has helped establish a blindness prevention program (www.hollows.org). Wanjiku loves the immediate impact of her work: today a patient is blind and, after an operation, tomorrow that patient can see. She also trains doctors in cataract surgery. Wanjiku tries to teach her three children to believe in God and that all things are possible.

> I do not want my life to be walled in or my spirit to be stifled. I want all possibilities, all encounters to be blown about my life as freely as possible. But I refuse to be blown off my feet in the pursuit of any.
>
> —Adapted from words of
> Mohandas Karamchand Gandhi

I have slightly adapted these words from the original quote by Gandhi. It is my favorite reflection because it reminds me that I can be whatever I want to be in this life and can interact with whomever I wish without the boundaries of discrimination.

I believe it is important for us all to embrace diversity whilst still sticking to our principles.

ELIZABETH MAY

Elizabeth May is the leader of the Green Party of Canada and a member of Parliament for Saanich-Gulf Islands in British Columbia. She is the first elected Green MP in the Canadian Parliament. Elizabeth is a well-known environmental lawyer and has been an activist for the last forty years in Canada. She holds three honorary doctorates, was a member of the Earth Charter Commission (www.earthcharterinaction.org), is an officer of the Order of Canada, and is the author of seven books.

> Let us return to the thought that life is a school. As one advances in school the tasks and examinations become more difficult. But the problems set by the Great Schoolmaster also become more meaningful and more to the point. Modern industry, by producing comfort on a scale unheard of in human history yet almost destroying the real educational function of daily work, quite clearly sets the most difficult examination task: how not to lose sight of the spiritual in the face of these overwhelming temptations...
>
> Out of the tremendous examination set by this monstrous development many single individuals will emerge triumphant; uncorrupted and hence incorruptible. This is all that really matters.
>
> This does not mean that we can wash our hands of this worldly failure; for only those can triumph who never cease for a moment, no

> matter what the odds are against them, to fight evil and try to restore order. "Woe unto the world because of offenses! for it must needs be that offenses come; but woe to that man by whom offense cometh!" (Mt 18:7). Anyone who merely "washes his hands" is one of those by whom offense comes.
>
> —E. F. Schumacher

There are so many inspirational pieces I could have chosen. Everything from St. Francis's prayer for serenity, to any one of a number of psalms, to the Tao of Pooh have all found their way into my own small book of accumulated prayers and reflections.

I chose this reading, one I first copied out into my journal thirty years ago, because I find it blends a keen understanding of the perils of our current consumer society with a practicing Christian's sense of moral purpose. Schumacher's work in economics, *Small Is Beautiful*, had an enormous influence on my life and work. Finding that he had a theological bent as well, expressed through such books as *Guide for the Perplexed* and the collected essays in *Good Work*, was, frankly, thrilling.

In the context of the current global climate crisis, the strength of purpose to continue to work, no matter what the odds against us, is seen as a spiritual imperative and not merely a practical calculation of how much good one can do, and it is as necessary as it is powerful.

RABBI MICHAEL MELCHIOR

Rabbi Michael Melchior is from Denmark where seven generations of his family were chief rabbis. He serves as a rabbi in Jerusalem and is still the chief rabbi of Norway's Jewish Community. In 1999 he was elected to the Knesset and served in various capacities as cabinet minister and in key roles in education, social affairs, environment, and Arab/Jewish relations. Today Rabbi Michael works in Israel through different movements and non-governmental organizations he has established, including the Mosaica Center for Inter-Religious Cooperation (www.mosaica-interreligious.org). The center is devoted to inter-religious dialogue and a framework for peace in Israel, the Palestinian Territories, and the Middle East.

> May he who makes peace in the heavens,
> make peace for us and for all Israel.
> And let us say, Amen.
>
> —Jewish prayer

This beautiful Jewish prayer is the text with which we conclude every single major prayer, the prayer we say three times a day—in the morning, the afternoon, and the evening—the prayer with which we conclude the grace after meals, the prayer that is used at both very happy and on very sad occasions (the Kaddish).

This prayer has also become a modern Hebrew folk song that is sung and danced to in circles far away from traditional observance of our religion.

The reason that I have chosen this prayer as my favorite is connected to the content: the intensive plea to G-d who makes peace in His heavens, that He may assist us in making peace for Israel, which really is an appeal to making peace on earth, because we believe that the peace of Israel can only be fully realized when all nations live in peace.

But my choice is also connected to a very special gesture we practice whenever we express this prayer. We physically withdraw three steps, symbolically saying to the Almighty that we cannot expect Him to intervene on our behalf in such a dramatic fashion if we ourselves are not willing to contribute to the realization of our dream, which symbolically means that we are willing to withdraw and leave room for the "Other."

This might be a naïve and romantic message, but I believe in it with all of my heart. It combines the knowledge that nothing can happen on earth without God wanting it, but also that we cannot just rely on the divine intervention but have to create the human vehicles and prepare the human hearts in order for this intervention to become efficient. I know of no better alternative in our world than an uncompromising commitment to making this prayer our reality.

AMJAD MOHAMED-SALEEM

Amjad Mohamed-Saleem is of Sri Lankan heritage and holds a Master's degree in civil and environmental engineering. He combined his practical skills and commitment to rebuilding communities when he was posted to Sri Lanka by Muslim Aid in 2004 to help oversee post-tsunami and post-conflict reconstruction. There he helped facilitate a unique and successful partnership between Muslim Aid and the US-based UMCOR (United Methodist Committee on Relief). Amjad is currently head of communications at The Cordoba Foundation, an independent research and public relations organization based in London, England. He contributes regularly to "paths2people," a forum that shares ideas and experiences and innovative ways of action (www.paths2people.com).

In the Name of God Most Gracious Most Merciful;

By the passing of time;

Verily Man is at loss;
Except those who have faith
And do righteous good deeds;
And enjoin upon each other,
The mutual teaching
Of truth and of
Patience and constancy.

—Qur'an 103

Why am I inspired by this passage? Because it reminds me that time cannot be wasted. As global leadership expert Robin Sharma says, "every second we dwell on the past, we steal from the future." Hence we should be focused on the present, whilst being aware of the past and future. We should not waste time, but be proactive in serving humanity and standing up for justice. For those of us who profess to have faith, it should be realized through our actions. We have to command the good, and enjoin truth. We should be patient and persistent.

This passage is a timely reminder that humanity has the right to have witnesses, living amongst us, who are willing to defend the truth no matter how unpopular it is. This prayer reminds me that until my last breath I will continue to do this, because I want to improve the quality of life of my fellow human beings.

DIDACIENNE MUKAHABESHIMANA

Rwandan Didacienne Mukahabeshimana was a nurse and trade unionist. When the genocide was over, Didacienne initially sought revenge on the perpetrators to gain inner peace. But after witnessing some public executions, she began her journey from hate to love. She asked God's forgiveness for her feelings of hate and asked that the perpetrators' souls rest in peace. Gradually many offenders came to trust Didacienne and her friends, recognizing their intention of love, and began writing letters to victims' families asking for forgiveness. In 2005, Didacienne co-founded UMUHUZA *(to rise above adversity), a non-governmental organization that teaches peace-making skills to people of all ages.*

Happy are those who know they are spiritually
poor; the Kingdom of heaven belongs to
them!
Happy are those who mourn; God will comfort
them!
Happy are those who are humble; they will
receive what God has promised!
Happy are those whose greatest desire is to do
what God requires: God will satisfy them
fully!
Happy are those who are merciful to others;
God will be merciful to them!
Happy are the pure in heart; they will see God!
Happy are those who work for peace; God will
call them his children!

Happy are those who are persecuted because
they do what God requires; the kingdom of
heaven belongs to them!
Happy are you when people insult you and
persecute you and tell all kinds of evil lies
against you because you are my followers.
Be happy and glad, for a great reward is kept for
you in heaven.
This is how the prophets who lived before you
were persecuted.

—Matthew 5:3–12

This passage, known as the Beatitudes, is inspirational for me. It is my constant strength during difficult situations and my guide to immortality.

My life is devoted to the Virgin Mary. She is my star who guides me to true happiness!

PROFESSOR DR. CHANDRA MUZAFFAR

Dr. Chandra Muzaffar is both a social activist and an academic. He is president of the International Movement for a Just World (JUST), an international non-governmental organization based in Malaysia that seeks to raise public consciousness on the moral and intellectual basis of global justice (www.just-international.org). Chandra is also chairman of the board of trustees of the 1Malaysia Foundation and is the Noordin Sopiee Professor of Global Studies at the Science University of Malaysia (USM) in Penang. He has published more than twenty books including Religion and Governance *and* Hegemony: Justice; Peace.

> I speak of plural souls in name alone–
> One soul becomes one hundred in their frames;
> Just as God's single sun in heaven
> shines on earth and lights a hundred walls
> But all these beams of light return to one
> if you remove the walls that block the sun
> The walls of houses do not stand forever
> and believers, then, will be as but one soul
>
> –Rumi

This poem, from the greatest mystic of all times, is a brilliant affirmation of the Oneness of God reflected in the oneness of creation and the oneness of the human family. It is this oneness that is our ultimate goal, our final destiny.

I chose this poem because it embodies my vision and my mission in life. Bringing people of different religions and cultures together on the basis of their common humanity has been my life's work. I have often argued that the similarities that bind us in terms of our common values and our shared interests are far more significant than the religious and cultural differences that separate us.

It is not just cultural and religious differences. There are other walls that keep us apart. Power, wealth, privilege, status, divide us even more.

But it has become more urgent than ever before to overcome these divisions and dichotomies. Technological and financial globalization has made us more interdependent. The environmental and economic crises that confront us today have underscored our interconnectedness. In other words, the realities of globalization and the grave challenges of our time have willy-nilly brought to the fore the eternal truth that Rumi reiterates: we are "one soul."

To bring to fruition this oneness, we have to struggle against all the iniquities and injustices, the barriers and the barricades that have fragmented the human family. This is why the struggle for the oneness of the human family is synonymous with the struggle for a just world.

DR. BAHIYYIH NAKHJAVANI

Bahiyyih Nakhjavani grew up in a family without borders. One grandfather was a Jew from Baghdad who now lies buried on a hill outside Kampala, Uganda. The other was a Caucasian Muslim from Baku who studied in Moscow and traveled to America before the Bolshevik Revolution. Bahiyyih has never known what nationality she belongs to and identifies herself by her Bahá'í beliefs rather than by her culture or her race. If there is a place she would call home, it would be the English language. A writer and a teacher, her novels include The Saddlebag, Paper, *and* The Woman Who Read Too Much.

The highest faculties which the learned have possessed, and whatsoever truths they, in their search after the gems of Thy knowledge, have discovered; the brightest realities with which the wise have been endowed, and whatever secrets they, in their attempts to fathom the mysteries of Thy wisdom, have unraveled, have all been created through the generative power of the Spirit that was breathed into the Pen which Thy hands have fashioned. How, then, can the thing which Thy Pen hath created be capable of comprehending those treasures of Thy Faith with which, as decreed by Thee, that Pen hath been invested? How can it ever know of the Fingers that grasp Thy Pen, and of Thy merciful favors with which it hath been endowed? How can it, already unable to reach this station, be made aware of the existence of Thy Hand that

> controlleth the Fingers of Thy might? How can it attain unto the comprehension of the nature of Thy Will that animateth the movement of Thy Hand?
>
> —Bahá'u'llah

This passage always incites wonder in me. It is a small part of a much longer prayer from the Bahá'i Writings and concerns our dawning spiritual awareness regarding the role and responsibility of the human soul in relation to the immensity of creation and its infinitely mysterious Source. But what I love most about it is the metaphor of writing it contains, the imagery of calligraphy it infers, and the idea of artistic composition on which it has been constructed.

I love the fact that it rises, layer after layer, on a rhetorical ladder of questions to which no answers can be given except in the very act of reading and of writing. I love the invitation it offers to contemplate multiple scales of motive and infinite layers of intention in the simple act of creation, even at the humblest level of words. It is like discovering all the stars of the Milky Way rolled up in a piece of flat paper and recognizing infinity in a single dot of ink.

PROFESSOR CHRISTOPHER O'BRIEN, AO

Australian Professor Chris O'Brien died in June 2009 after a long and valiant battle with a brain tumor. He was honored with a state funeral and was posthumously awarded an Officer in the Order of Australia (AO) for his services to medicine, as a surgeon, and to the community. He pioneered integrated, research-based, patient-centered, holistic cancer care in Australia. The Chris O'Brien Lifehouse at Royal Prince Alfred Hospital in Sydney is named in his honor and will be the largest facility of this kind in Australia (www.lifehouserpa.org.au).

Hail Mary, full of Grace,
The Lord is with thee,
Blessed art thou amongst women,
And blessed is the fruit of thy womb, Jesus.
Holy Mary, Mother of God,
Pray for us sinners now
And at the Hour of our death.
Amen.

—Hail Mary, traditional version

[Before his death, Chris O'Brien had agreed to contribute to A World of Prayer. *Gail O'Brien, Chris's wife, generously wrote and submitted this text after he died. Ed.]*

Having grown up Catholic, Chris returned to saying the rosary during his illness and gained great comfort from doing so. The former prime minister of Australia, Kevin Rudd, attended Mass with Chris in April 2009, two days after the launch of Lifehouse, and presented him with a gift of rosary beads which had been blessed and given to him by Pope Benedict XVI.

Chris treasured this gift and, in the last six weeks of his life, he prayed and taught me, who had grown up as a non-Catholic, to pray to the Blessed Virgin Mary with him.

Kevin Rudd said that through Chris's work in medicine, research, and fundraising, "his contribution to the community was massive, his work unceasing, his dedication to others without limit."

Chris was a much loved husband and father, and, always attentive and available, a doctor who was at ease with everyone he met. He knew how to make everyone feel important. It has been said that he became one with his patients through his illness and became accessible to all through his death.

CANON DR. PAUL OESTREICHER

Paul Oestreicher was born in Germany. At the age of seven, Paul and his parents fled Nazi Germany for New Zealand because his father's parents had been Jewish. After studying political science, Paul lived in England and trained as an Anglican priest. His life's work reflects his commitment to peace and human rights. He served as chair of Amnesty International UK from 1975 to 1979, director of the Centre for International Reconciliation, Coventry Cathedral, from 1986 to 1998, and vice president of the Campaign for Nuclear Disarmament. In retirement, Paul is Quaker Chaplain at the University of Sussex, England.

> ...we grasp at new forms and styles. And yet the suspicion remains; very few of us have the courage to measure our passion for moral change against the sacrifice of what lies closest to our hearts—our good name, our comfort, our security, our professional status.
>
> And yet, until such things are placed in jeopardy, nothing changes. The gospel says it; so do the times. Unless the cries of the war victims, the disenfranchised, the prisoners, the hopeless poor, the resisters of conscience...unless the cry of the world reaches our ears, and we measure our lives and deaths against those of others, nothing changes. Least of all ourselves; we stand like sticks and stones, impervious to the meaning of history or the cry of its Lord and Victim.
>
> —Daniel Berrigan, SJ

Written nearly forty years ago, this passage is no less true in the twenty-first century, true in the United States and true everywhere else. If Christians are to take Jesus seriously, living as he did, offering unconditional love and solidarity to all people, friend and foe, they will run into massive opposition, as Jesus did. They will suffer and yet be deeply enriched. Dan's brother Phil was in prison too. This letter was addressed to Dan's fellow Jesuits. It ends "I ask your prayers, that my brother and I and all who are at the edge, may be found faithful and obedient; in good humor and always at your side." From Dan and others like him in many parts of the world, I have learned that life at the edge is life somewhere near the heart of what Jesus called the Kingdom of God.

JACQUELINE OGEGA

Jackie Ogega has engaged in a wide range of work related to gender, international development, and peacebuilding. She is director of the Women's Mobilization Program at Religions for Peace International Secretariat in New York (www.religionsforpeace.org). She is the co-founder of Mpanzi, a rural organization dedicated to community peace (www.mpanzi.org). She also serves as an adjunct faculty member at the School for International Training in Vermont, USA. Her previous work in various positions in Africa focused on promoting peace, education, social justice, and the empowerment of women and girls. Her research interests include gender and peacebuilding, religion, identity, and social movements.

Today Jesus Wept
Watching a mother die
From the bullet of poverty
That stole her right
To give birth in safety
Surely
How could we yet again
Let a mother die giving life
As armies thrive taking life?

Today Jesus Wept
Listening to John confess
The rape of five-year-old Joyce
Not his first, but third count
Violating grandma, teenager, child
Surely

How could we yet again
Allow impunity to blossom
As we rip off bodies, souls and spirits?

Today Jesus wept
Watching the bomb explode
Trees, insects, animals, human limbs
All scattered away, turned to ashes
Skies and waters choked with smoke
Surely
How could we yet again
Divert resources to end malaria, TB, AIDS
As we wreak nuclear havoc on planet Earth?

—Jackie Ogega's reflections
based on "Jesus wept' (Jn 11:35)

If we reflect on the extent of world suffering, then we must be moved to tears. But tears are an outward expression of greater suffering and pain. We must remain much more deeply troubled in order to take concrete action that can end the rot and suffering. We do not have to be moved because we are directly impacted. The situation today calls on each one of us to work for the common good and in solidarity with the afflicted.

I think of the cases where women are dying during childbirth; the fact that rape in war and "peace" time is becoming normalized; that scores are dying of preventable diseases such as malaria, AIDS or tuberculosis. I dread the bombs and nuclear weapons. I am upset at the military expenditure and the resources spent on developing and spreading lethal technologies.

If only 2 percent of such budgets were directed to good causes, there would be fewer deaths and less poverty. Planet Earth is in peril. We are all called to be where suffering is happening in order to be moved to tears and, more deeply, to be mobilized to make a difference.

DR. EBOO PATEL

Named by U.S. News & World Report *as one of America's Best Leaders of 2009, Eboo Patel is the founder and president of Interfaith Youth Core (IFYC), a Chicago-based organization building the global interfaith youth movement (www.ifyc.org). Eboo, author of the award-winning book* Acts of Faith, *is also a regular contributor to the* Washington Post, USA Today, *and CNN. He served on President Obama's Advisory Council of the White House Office of Faith-Based and Neighborhood Partnership, and holds a doctorate in the sociology of religion from Oxford University, where he studied on a Rhodes scholarship.*

> We made you races and tribes for you to get to know each other.
>
> —Qur'an 49:13

One hundred years ago, the great African American scholar W. E. B. Du Bois said that the problem of the twentieth century would be the problem of the color line. Most people assumed that the color line divided black and white. But Dr. Martin Luther King Jr. suggested that the real dividing line was between those who wanted to live together as brothers and those who wanted to perish together as fools.

I believe the twenty-first century will be dominated by the question of the *faith line*. Our first and most important challenge is to recognize that the faith line does not divide Muslims from Christians, Hindus from Buddhists, or secularists from the faithful. The faith line separates those who believe in pluralism from those who believe religions are fated to fight. In today's world, where people from different backgrounds interact at a higher frequency and intensity than ever before, we have to ensure these interactions lead to cooperation rather than this conflict that some would say is inevitable.

This is my inspiration for Interfaith Youth Core, an organization I started about a decade ago to make real the hope, expressed in this Surah (chapter), that we can live together in equal dignity and mutual loyalty. At IFYC, we believe young interfaith leaders can build bridges of cooperation rather than barriers of division between religions. We train and nurture these young people to lead projects that bring diverse groups together around the common good and encourage them to ask one another, "*What from your tradition inspires you to serve?*" My response is often this Surah, which shows that pluralism is a deeply rooted value in Islam, as it is in America, and in other traditions.

ZOYA PHAN

Zoya Phan is from the Karen ethnic group in Burma. When she was fourteen, Burmese army soldiers attacked her village, forcing Zoya and her family to flee. They hid in the jungle for weeks before finding their way to a refugee camp in Thailand. She is now a refugee living in London, working as the international coordinator at Burma Campaign UK (www.burmacampaign.org.uk). She has met with former British Prime Minister Gordon Brown and other world politicians, urging them to take action on Burma. Her autobiography, Little Daughter: A Memoir of Survival in Burma and the West, *describes the ongoing suffering of the Karen in Burma.*

O my beloved daughter,
In the long journey of life,
In broad daylight, under the sun,
As it's hard to know where north and south are,
There're also those who're standing still.

Though in the middle of the night,
A time hard to see the way,
As north and south are definitely known,
There're those who're journeying towards the destination.

In the stormy wind,
And the waves blasting,
Crying and wailing,
In abandonment,
There're also those who've sunk into depravity.

In the violent storm,
And the stormy sea,
There're also those who are journeying,
Against the current and vicious wind.

O my beloved daughter,
Keep sincerity and conscience,
Alertness and ethics,
Diligence and learning,
Faith and uprightness,
Courage and sacrifice,
As a base and journey on,
With fearlessness,
For the noble cause.

—Padoh Mahn Sha Lah Phan

This poem was written by my father and dedicated to all women in Burma. I chose it in memory of my father (Padoh Mahn Sha Lah Phan) and my mother (Nant Kyin Shwe) who were both caring and loving parents not just for their children but for all the people in Burma. Both my father and mother dedicated their lives to freedom for Burma and I am proud to be their daughter. My father and mother may be dead but, as their daughter, I will continue their dedicated work toward true freedom for my people and peace in my country. The Karen and the people in Burma will one day be free.

DR. JENNY PLANE TE PAA

Jenny Plane Te Paa remains the first and only long serving lay indigenous Anglican seminary dean in the world. She is widely recognized as a significant and fearless global Anglican lay leader for her work in theological education, in peace and justice advocacy, in promoting women's ministry leadership, in supporting indigenous struggles, and in campaigning for inclusive church. Jenny lives in Auckland, New Zealand. She enjoys being a devoted grandmother, mother, sister, daughter, and friend to many.

> In religion as in all else truth is not prized less highly because it is no longer fenced on any side.
>
> We are living in a new world: it is ours, if we are true to the faith that is in us, to seek to make it a better world. It is by prayer and service that we may hope to do it... New knowledge and new ways of life bring with them new customs and forms of speech unknown before. As men [and women] think upon God's wonderful works unveiled before them and are quickened afresh by the power of [God's] Spirit, their hearts and minds frame for themselves new prayers and thanksgivings and seek new occasions of worship... In all things we have set before our eyes the duty of faithfulness to the teaching of Scripture and the godly and decent order of the ancient Fathers, and we pray that by God's blessing upon our work those who use this book

may be enabled to keep the unity of the Spirit in the bond of peace.

—Preface to the 1928
Book of Common Prayer (BCP)

As with many of my indigenous sisters and brothers, I stand in the complex legacy of the colonizing missionising project which began in the nineteenth century. Church Mission Society missionaries first arrived and were generously cared for by Maori and to this day most indigenous Maoris are Anglican. Apart from the Bible and the sacraments, my most abiding ecclesial treasure is the 1662 *Book of Common Prayer*. When I was a child, my worship was heavily influenced by my grandfather and other elders from whom I learned to pray, grieve, heal, inspire, sing, and offer comfort. As I grew older, I began to question the injustices experienced by my ancestors and the complicity of the Church and I wondered how faith in a God of mercy could remain so unflinching. Time and again my grandfather would reassure me that within *Te Paipera* (the Bible) and *Te Rawiri* (the *Book of Common Prayer*) lay all the answers!

It was during my PhD years that I came across the words I have submitted from the preface of my grandfather's 1928 BCP. For me they encapsulate the sheer goodness of heart, simplicity of spirit, and depth of intellect that resonated in my elders as they sought to be good and faithful servants of God. Nothing distracted them from their unshakable faith, from their task of teaching and nurturing responsibilities for future. As I reflect on the words in the Preface, I am reminded to be appropriately obedient to traditions handed down even as I am encouraged to consider the time and circumstances for which they were intended.

I am blessed to belong to *te whanau a te Karaiti* (the family of Christ) in the land of my birth, in the land of my ancestors, and to now stand in the faith-filled footsteps of my elders. I am blessed at being entrusted with the responsibility of continuing the struggle for God's justice. I do so with confidence and in full assurance that we are indeed "living in a new world: it is ours, if we are true to the faith that is in us, to seek to make it a better world. It is by prayer and service that we may hope to do it."

CANON PATIENCE PURCHAS

Patience Purchas is a retired Church of England priest. After fourteen years in ministry and many years campaigning, in 1994 she was one of the first women to be ordained a priest in England. In addition to working in religious broadcasting and adult education she has as director of ordinands, worked closely with people who were exploring their sense of vocation. Patience was a member of the bishop of St. Albans Senior Staff and the General Synod. She has written two devotional books and contributed chapters to a number of others. She is a wife and mother and has five grandchildren.

> He did not say: You will not be troubled, you will not be belabored, you will not be disquieted; but he said: You will not be overcome. God wants us to pay attention to these words, and always to be strong in faithful trust, in well-being and in woe, for he loves us and delights in us, and so he wishes us to love him and delight in him and trust greatly in him, and all will be well.
>
> —Julian of Norwich

These words from the *Revelations of Divine Love* were written by a woman anchorite or hermit, Dame Julian of Norwich, in the fifteenth century. I was given a copy of the *Revelations* or *Shewings* [*Showings*], as she herself called them, as a teenager. It was during the sometimes testing years leading up to the decision to allow women to be ordained as priests in the Church of England that I came to value this particular passage.

The Christian faith has never taught that life will be a bed of roses. What it promises is that we shall be given bread for the journey and that we never travel alone. In the end, all shall be well.

FR. TIMOTHY RADCLIFFE, OP

Timothy Radcliffe joined the Dominican Order (The Order of Preachers) in 1965, taught theology at Oxford, and was elected master of the order in 1992. He has written several books, including What Is the Point of Being a Christian? *and* Why Go to Church? The Drama of the Eucharist. *He has been involved in the peace movement and in care for people with AIDS and is an itinerant preacher. Fr. Timothy is also a trustee with CAFOD, the Catholic Agency for Overseas Development (www.cafod.org.uk).*

> Late have I loved you, O beauty so ancient and so new; late have I loved you!... For behold you were within me, and I outside... You called and cried to me and broke open my deafness and you sent forth your beams and shone upon me and chased away my blindness; you breathed fragrance upon me and I drew in my breath and now I pant for you: I tasted you, and now hunger and thirst for you. You touched me, and I have burned for your peace.
>
> —Saint Augustine

I love this prayer because it is passionate. It is also very bodily, referring to all our senses: hearing, sight, smell, taste, and touch. Often religion can be a bloodless thing, but here we see the spiritual penetrating all of our bodily existence. We can best share our faith with our contemporaries through beauty, which breaks through all barriers and gives us a glimpse of our ultimate happiness.

TARIQ RAMADAN

Tariq Ramadan holds a Master's degree in philosophy and French literature and a PhD in Arabic and Islamic studies. In Egypt, he trained in classical Islamic scholarship at Al-Azhar University. Currently he is professor of contemporary Islamic studies at Oxford University, a visiting professor in Qatar and Morocco, and a senior research fellow at Doshisha University in Japan. Tariq Ramadan is also president of the European Muslim Network. He has contributed significantly to the debate on contemporary Islamic issues, Islamic revival in the world, and Muslims in the West. He is author of many books, and he lectures extensively throughout the world on theology, ethics, interfaith and intercultural dialogue (www.tariqramadan.com).

> O God, we ask you to provide us with God-consciousness, human detachment, spiritual richness and love of the poor.
>
> —Al-Bukhari Collection of prophetic traditions

I have chosen a very short prayer that comes from Islamic prophetic tradition. It translates from Arabic to English roughly as this. Although it is short, I believe that it encompasses all dimensions that are essential for a spiritual life.

First, I believe that God-consciousness is important. This is the sense of God's closeness, his proximity—where he is much more a companion *for me* than a judge *of me*. There is a saying in the Qur'an that the knowledge of God is between you and your heart. So this gives meaning to my life, and indeed any life.

Second, human detachment reminds us that at the end of the day it is important to know your priorities. This detachment can be used to help us as human beings to recognize the things within our lives that are not essential and have detachment from them. I believe that this reminder is especially important in our world today with all its emphasis on consumerism. Detachment can also remind us of the struggle for justice.

The third part of the prayer, spiritual richness, comes from the first two. This capacity to give is to know the understanding of fulfillment from spiritual richness. It is being free from material dimensions.

Fourth, we ask for love of the poor. This is for us to both love and be loved by the poor. I believe that to be close to the first dimension within this prayer, that is, God, you have to be close to the last, the poor.

For me, this prayer encapsulates the meaning of a spiritual life, the meaning of what I can ask, and it can be summarized quite simply as "light." Indeed within all the major faiths, Hinduism, Buddhism, Judaism, Christianity, and Islam, these four concepts—God, detachment, spiritual richness and generosity—are all recognized as "light." That is to say, "God gives us more light, deeper discernment."

CHRISTINA REES

Christina Rees is a writer and broadcaster and has worked for many years for women's inclusion in the ordained ministries of the Church of England. She was chair of Women and the Church (WATCH) for more than thirteen years (www.womenandthechurch.org) and is the vice chair of the Li Tim-Oi Foundation. Christina has been a member of General Synod since 1990. She speaks and preaches widely and is also a communications trainer and consultant. Born in America and raised on a boat in the Caribbean and Mediterranean Seas, Christina lives on a small holding in England, where she has raised a family and many rare breeds of animals.

From the time that it was shown I desired often to know what was our Lord's meaning. And fifteen years after and more, I was answered in inward understanding, saying, "Would you know your Lord's meaning in this? Learn it well. Love was his meaning. Who showed it you? Love. What did he show you? Love. Why did he show you? For love. Hold fast to this, and you shall learn and know more about love, but you will never need to know or understand about anything else for ever and ever." Thus did I learn that love was our Lord's meaning.

And so I saw full surely that before ever God made us, he loved us. And this love was never quenched nor ever shall be. And in this love he has done all his works, and in this love he has made all things profitable to us, and in this love

> our life is everlasting. In our making we had beginning, but the love in which he made us was in him from without beginning, in which love we have our beginning.
>
> —Julian of Norwich

This sublime and transcendent passage was written over six hundred years ago by Mother Julian, a woman who, on May 8, 1373, when she was thirty years old and gravely ill, had a series of sixteen intense visions of the Holy Trinity, and in particular, the person of Jesus Christ. She became instantly well and spent the next twenty years of her life meditating on these visions, or "Shewings" [Showings] as she called them.

The book she wrote as a result of her extraordinary experience, *Revelations of Divine Love*, was the first book to be written in English by a woman. After her miraculous healing, she became an anchoress (a woman dedicated to religion, living permanently alone) and lived for many years in a room attached to a little church in Norwich, Norfolk, England, where people would come seeking her wisdom and advice.

Mother Julian, with her passionate vision of God's love and delight in us, is one of my favorite theologians. She expresses more beautifully than any other writer the tenderness and compassion of Christ. She is also the author of perhaps the most exquisitely confident and encouraging words outside the Bible: "All shall be well, and all shall be well, and all manner of thing shall be well."

SOGYAL RINPOCHE

Sogyal Rinpoche is a world-renowned Buddhist teacher from Tibet and author of the highly acclaimed The Tibetan Book of Living and Dying. *He is also the founder and spiritual director of Rigpa, an international network of Buddhist centers and groups (www.rigpa.org). Rigpa aims to present the Buddhist tradition of Tibet in a way that is both completely authentic and as relevant as possible to the lives and needs of modern men and women. Today, Rigpa has more than one hundred and thirty centers and groups in forty-one countries around the world.*

For as long as space exists
And sentient beings endure,
May I too remain,
To dispel the misery of the world.

—Shantideva

Lord, make me an instrument of thy peace.
Where there is hatred, Let me sow love;
Where there is injury, pardon;
Where there is doubt, faith;
Where there is despair, hope;
And where there is sadness, joy.
O Divine Master, grant that
I may not so much seek
To be consoled as to console;
To be understood as to understand;
To be loved as to love;
For it is in giving that we receive,

It is in pardoning that we are pardoned,
And it is in dying that we are born to eternal life.
—Attributed to St. Francis of Assisi

I have chosen these prayers because they capture the essence of love, compassion, and altruism that lie at the heart of all the great spiritual traditions. The words from these two great traditions—one Buddhist and one Christian—seem to come from the same source and convey the enactment of compassion at the most profound level. The most powerful prayers are the ones that touch, inspire, and bring out the best in us, the goodness that we all have, as Buddhists call it, *bodhichitta*, or the heart of the enlightened mind. If we can truly embody the meaning of these great prayers, we can bring such benefit, both to ourselves and to others.

PATRICIA ROBERTS

Patricia Roberts is a Christian Taoist, a spiritual director, and a Tai Ji teacher (www.sdiworld.org). Patricia was born and raised in Arequipa, Peru, and after thirty years of living in the United States and six years in Spain, she is now back home. From there, Patricia travels around the world offering her seminar, "The Dance of Life," which integrates Lectio Divina, centering prayer, and Tai Ji in a dance of harmony and reconciliation. Patricia also offers spiritual tourism, taking groups for contemplative/Tai Ji experiences in the highlands of Peru all the way to Machu Picchu.

Blessed be the light of day and the Lord who
sends it to us.

In this new day we give you thanks Omnipotent
God, Master of the Universe.

Your divine kindness has brought us out of the
night darkness
into the light of a new day. Everything in the
world is filled with your glory.

Because of you, flowers bloom, fields turn green,
trees produce fruits and we receive the rays
of sun.

Birds in the branches bless you as well as the fish
in the ponds.

Bless us great God and guide our steps,
so that we may forever abide by your holy
law. In this new day, we give you thanks
Omnipotent God, Master of creation.

—Rosa Victoria Calderón de Billig

This prayer was taught to me by my grandmother. She awoke me to the beauty of creation and the harmony of living with right relationships in gratefulness. I have since passed this prayer on to my children and grandchildren.

I discovered Taoism through Chungliang Al Huang [whose contribution to this book appears on page 3], a renowned Tai Ji master, who taught me to embody the awareness that my grandmother had instilled in me and to be part of the natural world. In addition, he taught me to be a manifestation of the Great Mystery according to the form I have been given and to allow the ebb and flow in my relationships with my community, the planet, and myself without renouncing the Christian tradition. The German mystic and theologian Meister Eckhart was also a great inspiration to me.

FR. RICHARD ROHR, OFM

Father Richard Rohr is a Franciscan of the New Mexico Province. He became founding director of the Center for Action and Contemplation in Albuquerque, New Mexico in 1986, and considers the proclamation of the gospel to be his primary call. In communicating this message he uses different platforms, including scripture as liberation, the integration of action and contemplation, community building, peace and justice issues, male spirituality, and eco-spirituality. Living in a hermitage near his Albuquerque Franciscan community, Fr. Richard writes daily meditations, and a newsletter called Radical Grace. *He has also has published many books (www.cacradicalgrace.org).*

God of the Ages,
Christ, the Alpha and the Omega of history,
Holy Spirit, You who fill and connect all things,
We know that in You a thousand years are a
single day,
And a single day is a thousand years.

Your today does not give way to tomorrow,
Your now does not follow yesterday,
You Live in the eternal present,
where all things are one, and forgiven,
and surrounded by mercy

We who are caught in the flux of time,
Seek to be where You are.
We seek to be present to Your Eternal
Presence–

where all is one, forgiven,
and surrounded by mercy.
Amen.

—Richard Rohr, OFM

Perhaps no generation of humanity has been more prepared to see time in a new way than our own. The early allusion to time in the prayer, "a thousand years are a single day..." is from Psalm 90:4 and 2 Peter 3. It tells us that from God's perspective time is a total illusion with one day and a thousand years being interchangeable. We alone live in what feels like past, present, and future. Yet Albert Einstein and modern physics have helped us to understand that space and time are completely relative to one another (as if we could "understand" this!), and that the only constant in the universe seems to be the speed of light.

God lives and creates us inside this Eternal Light that God is. When we allow ourselves to sink into this Mystery, all notions of reward and punishment, fear and anxiety fade inside an all-embracing compassion and mercy. One cannot teach this or prove this to anyone: people have to "fall" into this timeless Love for themselves, and then they know. Every human love, and every moment of awe and wonder, is an invitation and a promise of this eternal now.

RABBI DR. DAVID ROSEN, CBE, KSG

David Rosen is the former chief rabbi of Ireland and is currently the Jerusalem-based international director of interreligious affairs of the American Jewish Committee (AJC). He is also the honorary advisor on interreligious affairs to the Chief Rabbinate of Israel. He is the past chairman of the International Jewish Committee for Interreligious Consultations (IJCIC) that represents World Jewry to other world religions and is an international co-president of Religions for Peace.

Lord of Peace, Divine Ruler, to whom peace belongs!
Master of Peace, Creator of all things!

May it be thy will to put an end to war and bloodshed on earth, and to spread a great and wonderful peace over the whole world, so that nation shall not lift up sword against nation, neither shall they learn war anymore.

Help us and save us all, and let us cling tightly to the virtue of peace. Let there be a truly great peace between every person and their fellow, and between husband and wife, and let there be no discord between people even in their hearts.

Let us never shame any person on earth, great or small. May it be granted unto us to fulfill Thy Commandment to "*Love thy neighbor as thyself,"* with all our hearts and souls and bodies and possessions.

And let it come to pass in our time as it is written, *"And I will give peace in the land, and you shall lie down and none shall make you afraid. I will drive the wild beasts from the land, and neither shall the sword go through your land."*

God who is peace, bless us with peace!

—A Jewish Peace Prayer attributed to Rabbi Nachman ben Feiga of Breslov

I chose this prayer for peace because it is indeed a lovely prayer and expresses some of my deepest hopes and aspirations. Moreover it expresses the universality that is the authentic expression of Jewishness but which, for historical reasons, has often been stifled by the situations Jews have found themselves in. Indeed, precisely because conditions for Jews at the time and in the place it was written were far from happy, the prayer is impressive in reflecting the universal moral consciousness to which authentic Judaism aspires.

ZAINAB SALBI

Zainab Salbi grew up under Saddam Hussein's regime. Stranded in America because of the Gulf War, Zainab later founded Women for Women International (WFWI), a humanitarian organization that helps women survivors of wars rebuild their lives (www.womenforwomen.org). Since 1993, WFWI has provided economic and emotional aid, to nearly three hundred thousand women from Bosnia and Herzegovina, Rwanda, Afghanistan, Iraq, and Sudan. Zainab is author of two books, recipient of many awards, and a World Economic Forum Young Global Leader. WFWI was awarded the 2006 Conrad N. Hilton Humanitarian Prize. It was the first women's organization to receive this honor.

Out beyond ideas of wrongdoing and rightdoing,
there is a field. I'll meet you there.

When the soul lies down in that grass,
The world is too full to talk about.
Ideas, language, even the phrase *each other*
doesn't make any sense

—Jalâl al-Din Rumi, "Out Beyond Ideas"

Dance, when you're broken open.
Dance, if you've torn the bandage off.
Dance in the middle of the fighting.
Dance in your blood.
Dance, when you're perfectly free.

—Jalâl al-Din Rumi, "Dance"

These poems inspired me to write my memoir, *Between Two Worlds: Escape from Tyranny: Growing Up in the Shadow of Saddam*. By writing and talking about my truth, I was able to be healed and be transformed.

I chose the first poem because I believe in the oneness of humanity. In order to see this oneness, we need to build bridges between the different worlds that we come from, bridges that show our common humanity in its beauty and horror, its generosity and greed and its masculine and feminine.

I chose the second poem because I believe in the power of joy. We do ourselves the biggest injustice when we deprive ourselves of joy, because through it we can see all the beauty in small things and big things such as caterpillars and butterflies. It is through the eyes of joy that we can appreciate the fullness of this world's generosity and the giving of Mother Earth. It is through joy that we can overcome our challenges and celebrate all experiences. It is joy that makes me grateful for all I have been through and all that I have become and may still become. It is with joy that I choose to live.

SWAMI NIRANJAN SARASWATI

Swami Niranjan Saraswati is the disciple of and spiritual successor to the yoga master Sri Swami Satyananda Saraswati. In 1964, at the age of four, Swami Niranjan joined the Bihar School of Yoga, where he would eventually serve as president from 1983 to 2008. In 1990, he was initiated as a paramahamsa sannyasin *(a group of ascetics who focus on the practice of yoga). He founded Bihar Yoga Bharati, the first university of yoga, and also Bal Yoga Mitra Mandal, a children's yoga movement with over one hundred thousand members. A magnetic source of wisdom and author of many classic books on yoga, tantra, and the Upanishads, Swami Niranjan continues to nurture his guru's mission from his base at Munger, Bihar, India.*

I am an invisible child of a thousand faces of
 love
That floats over the swirling sea of life,
Surrounded by the meadows of the winged
 shepherds,
Where stillness of divine love and beauty
Rain in the spring and bloom at midnight
Summer's warmth of softness...
I know that I am untouchable to the forces
As long as I have a direction, an aim, a goal:
To serve, to love, and to give...
If I believe I have the strength
To hold back seas, to move mountains,
And the determination to live and love life,
It is because I have felt and seen an image of
 inspiration

Visible to my unseeing eyes...
But never shall I run or turn from life, from me.
Never shall I forsake myself
Or the timeless lessons I have taught myself,
Nor shall I let the value
Of divine inspiration and being be lost.
My rainbow-colored bubble
Will carry me further than beyond the horizon's
settings,
Forever to serve, to love, and to live
As a sannyasin.

—Swami Satyananda Saraswati

This favorite poem, by my guru, Sri Swami Satyananda Saraswati, highlights *sankalpa*, or positive affirmation, and focuses on the will and the energies of the mind and spirit to attain a goal. It is a process of training the mind to develop the will and clarity of thought. Sankalpa is not just a wish, but a conviction. It is trust and faith in oneself, in one's own strength and courage: "*I have that: therefore I can become that.*"

The sankalpa of a saint or sannyasin is a living force, held in the heart and expressed in every thought and deed. Through dedication and constant effort to rise above the mundane to the heights of spiritual consciousness, through offering oneself in service to others, over time, the energy of the sankalpa crystallizes, becoming a tangible force that intensifies in power. That is why it is said that a sannyasin can change the vision of the world.

PETE SEEGER

Pete Seeger is a beloved American folk singer of protest music in support of international disarmament, civil rights, and for environmental causes. His best known songs include "Where Have All the Flowers Gone?" "If I Had a Hammer" (composed with Lee Hays), and "Turn, Turn, Turn!" He was one of the folksingers most responsible for popularizing the spiritual "We Shall Overcome," which became the acknowledged anthem of the 1960s American Civil Rights Movement. More recently he has supported the Hudson River Sloop Clearwater (www.clearwater.org), a non-profit organization created to preserve and protect the Hudson River.

All people that on earth do dwell,
Sing out for peace 'tween heav'n and hell.
'Tween East and West and low and high,
Sing! peace on earth and sea and sky.

Old Hundred, you've served many years
To sing one people's hopes and fears,
But we've new verses for you now.
Sing peace between the earth and plow.

Sing peace between the grass and trees,
Between the continents and seas,
Between the lion and the lamb.
Between young Ivan and young Sam.

Between the white, black, red and brown,
Between the wilderness and town,

Sing peace between the near and far,
'Tween Allah and six pointed star.

The fish that swim, the birds that fly,
The deepest seas, the stars on high,
Bear witness now that you and I
Sing peace on earth and sea and sky.

Old Hundred, please don't think us wrong
For adding verses to your song.
Sing peace between the old and young,
'Tween every faith and every tongue.

—Pete Seeger

This song, "Old Hundred," is based on Psalm 100 and is sung to the tune of the hymn "All People That on Earth Do Dwell."

RULA SHUBEITA

Rula Shubeita is a Christian Arab Palestinian living in Jerusalem. Originally a teacher, she now works primarily as a tourist guide with Christian pilgrims from all over the world. In 2010 she established her own travel agency, Good News Tours. Rula's profession is her ministry: witnessing to the Bible and Christian spirituality in the Holy Land and bringing alive the three Abrahamic religions: Judaism, Christianity, and Islam. Rula frequently participates in interreligious delegations both in Israel and overseas. Through her ministry, Rula is committed to celebrating humanity's similarities and differences expressed in different cultures and traditions. She believes that justice, reconciliation, peace, and love are fundamental to living in our world today.

Angel of God,
my guardian dear,
to whom God's love commits me here,
ever this day, be at my side
to light and guard,
to rule and guide.

— Traditional Catholic prayer

My mother taught me this short prayer when I was three years old and it is still with me. I recite it every night in Arabic (my first language) before I go to sleep and also in the morning. It makes me feel strong all day long. I also recite it when I think I am in danger, when I walk, when I drive, and during any unusual activity. It really works. I believe my angel is always with me.

HIS HOLINESS SANT RAJINDER SINGH JI MAHARAJ

His Holiness Sant Rajinder Singh Ji Maharaj is a leading spiritual master, teaching meditation on the inner Light and Sound. He is head of Science of Spirituality—Sawan Kirpal Ruhani Mission, a non-profit, non-denominational organization devoted to teaching meditation to achieve peace, unity, and love (www.sos.org). He is also president of the Human Unity Conference and the Seventh World Religions Conference. A best-selling author of numerous books on meditation and spirituality, his books, which include Inner and Outer Peace through Meditation *and* Empowering Your Soul through Meditation, *have been published in fifty languages. He travels the world teaching meditation and his talks are broadcast on television, radio, and the Internet.*

Let this world become a temple of love and peace.
Let love and Truth illumine the world,
And the adversaries of peace awaken to its Light.
This sacred land of God has been trampled with
 the burden of oppression.
Life is not a dagger stained with the blood of hatred;
It is a branch filled with the flowers of love and
 compassion.

Life itself is restless for peace in the world.
Let its noble dream materialize.
May the garden be illumined with wave after
 wave of Light.
May the wealth of love grow greater and greater
 and enrich every heart.

—Sant Darshan Singh Ji Maharaj

The verses that capture the essence of what I consider the purpose of life and have been the inspiration of my life are those by the great poet-saint Sant Darshan Singh Ji Maharaj, a past master of meditation on the inner Light and Sound. His penetrating words illumine the path anyone can take to achieve peace through uncovering the Divine within. This transcendent peace, once it permeates our being, can spread to others and bathe this planet in peace.

These verses describe the unity at the heart of all creation. The poet realizes that the same Light of God within us is also in all others, making us one family of God. When we realize we are all one family, we would not cause pain or suffering to others. As we would not want to hurt our parents or children, we would not want to hurt any other human being. The walls that divide us through nationality, religion, social status, or appearance come tumbling down as we realize that we are all children of the one Parent—God.

We can have a firsthand experience of our unity through meditation on the inner Light and Sound within each. Through absorption into this Light and Sound current, we experience consciousness of higher spiritual realms. This inner journey leads back to the source of this current and we experience oneness with the Creator. Then, we recognize that all humans and all forms of life are created by God and comprise one family. This nondenominational meditation practice can be performed by people of all religions and nationalities. Spiritual progress is enhanced by an ethical life of non-violence, truthfulness, humility, love for all, and selfless service.

As we gaze at the wonders within through meditation, we can experience the inner Light, enjoy its nourishing peace and bliss, and radiate that loving luminosity to all.

BHAI SAHIB BHAI (DR.) MOHINDER SINGH

Bhai Sahib Bhai (Dr.) Mohinder Singh is third in line of spiritual leaders and chairman of the Sikh charity, Guru Nanak Nishkam Sewak Jatha (GNNSJ) in Birmingham, United Kingdom. Its award-winning "Nishkam" projects promote partnership and innovation through shared values and responsibility, both locally and globally. "Bhai Sahib Bhai" is a rare and prestigious Sikh title, acknowledging his historic contributions in intra-faith and interfaith cooperation. Bhai Sahib is also recognized internationally as an interfaith visionary, and has received the Juliet Hollister Award from the Temple of Understanding. He holds two honorary doctorates from Birmingham's universities and has advised city schools on values-centered education.

> Recognize the entire human race as one family. The Transcendent is known by different names. Karta (the Creator) and Karim (the Merciful) is one and the same; so too is Razak (the Sustainer) and Rahim (the Compassionate).
>
> —*Sri Dasam Granth*, attributed to
> Sri Guru Gobind Singh Ji, the tenth Sikh Guru

> The whole world is suffering, engulfed in the flames of many destructive forces. We plead to you God—through Your mercy please protect and save us. No matter which door or sanctuary or place of worship we come from, take us into Your refuge and shelter and rescue us.
>
> —*Sri Guru Granth Sahib*, 853,
> Guru Amar Das, the third Sikh Guru

> Where there is spiritual wisdom there is righteousness and Dharam (faith); where there is falsehood there is sin; where there is greed, there is death and destruction; and where there is forgiveness there is God Himself.
>
> —*Sri Guru Granth Sahib*, 1372,
> Bhagat Kabir, renowned saint of India

The Sikh *Dharam* (faith) was founded by ten successive Sikh Gurus between 1469 and 1708, after which the scripture was elevated to the status of Guru—*Sri Guru Granth Sahib*. Its verses—including those of Hindu and Muslim saints as well as the Sikh Gurus—rest on one enduring conviction: *Ik Oankar*—that there is but only One Creator, omnipresent, eternal and all-embracing.

Translations are but a poor substitute for any original scriptural text. The English versions offered here convey a vital message—to accept diversity, and achieve collective strength through unity. We exist in an infinitely vast context; how foolish then is our arrogance and how precious the qualities of wisdom, humility, and solidarity.

The first prayer underscores the oneness of humanity. Amidst the panorama of different identities and traditions, our differences are, ultimately, illusory. To live "in God's image" is to emulate godly virtues and realize our shared identity as sparks of the same divine flame. The second prayer is construed as a plea from us humans to the Universal Creator; the world is aflame; whosoever or wheresoever we may come from, forgive us and save us, by whatever means. The final prayer takes us further toward that most challenging and healing of qualities—one could say, to the heart of God: "where there is greed, there is death and destruction, and where there is forgiveness—there is God Himself."

DR. HUSTON SMITH

Dr. Huston Smith was born to missionary parents in China in 1919. His lifelong spiritual journey led him to meet many people who shaped twentieth-century spiritual America, including Martin Luther King, Jr. and Thomas Merton. He practiced Vedanta Hinduism, Sufism, and Zen Buddhism for many years and discovered Tibetan multiphonic chanting. He is author of fourteen books, including his seminal work The World's Religions. *He taught philosophy and religious studies for many years and is currently Thomas J. Watson Professor of Religion and Distinguished Adjunct Professor of Philosophy, Emeritus, Syracuse University.*

Om asato ma sad gamaya,
tamaso ma jyotir gamaya,
mrityor ma amritam gamaya

Om shantih shantih shantih

Lead me from the unreal to the Real
Lead me from darkness to Light
Lead me from death to Immortality.

Peace, peace, peace.

—Hindu Sanskrit chant,
with additional invocation
("Peace peace, peace") from Dr. Smith

I believe the importance of this prayer is obvious and requires no explanation.

THE RIGHT REVEREND JOHN S. SPONG

John Shelby Spong was bishop of the Episcopal Diocese of Newark from 1976 to 2000. A preeminent voice for liberal Christianity, he is a lecturer and author of twenty-four books that have sold over one million copies. They include A New Christianity of the World, Jesus for the Non Religious, *and his autobiography*, Here I Stand: My Struggle for a Christianity of Integrity, Love, and Equality. *He has several honorary degrees and was named Quatercentenary Scholar by Cambridge University (Emmanuel College) in 1992 (www.johnshelbyspong.com).*

Look at him!
Look not at his divinity,
but look, rather, at his freedom.
Look not at the exaggerated tales of his power,
but look, rather, at his infinite capacity to
give himself away.
Look not at the first-century mythology that
surrounds him,
but look, rather, at his courage to be,
his ability to live,
the contagious quality of his love.

Stop your frantic search!
Be still and know that this is God:
this love,
this freedom,
this life,
this being;

and
when you are accepted,
accept yourself;
when you are forgiven,
forgive yourself;
when you are loved,
love yourself.
Grasp that Christpower
and
dare to be yourself!

—John S. Spong

In my attempt to separate the essence of the Christ from the interpretive creeds, doctrines, and dogmas of the Church, this poem has been the basis for my studies and spiritual journey for the last thirty years.

REVEREND HELEN SUMMERS

Reverend Helen Summers has devoted much of her professional life to education and religious and spiritual studies. She was a lecturer in Australian universities and has designed programs for Aboriginal senior men and women. In 1997, Helen graduated from The New Seminary for Interfaith Ministers and, seeing the need to promote religious and spiritual understanding among multicultural communities in Victoria, founded the Interfaith Centre of Melbourne (www.interfaithcentre.org.au). Her interfaith collaborations include serving as a board member of the 2009 Melbourne Parliament of the World's Religions, producing the exhibition Breaking the Veils: Women Artists from the Islamic World, and coordinating Ten Promises to Peace, an evening with Yusuf Islam (Cat Stevens).

May the fire be in our thoughts
Making them true, good and just,
May it protect us from the evil one.

May the fire be in our eyes;
May it open our eyes to share what is good in life.
We ask that the fire may protect us from what
Is not rightfully ours.

May the fire be on our lips, so that we may
Speak the truth in kindness; that we may serve
and encourage others.
May it protect us from speaking evil.

May the fire be in our ears.
We pray that we may hear with a deep, deep listening

So that we may hear the flow of water, and of all
Creation.
And the dreaming.
May we be protected from gossip and from things
That harm and break down our family.

May the fire be in our arms and hands
So that we may be of service and build up love.
May the fire protect us from all violence.

May the fire be in our whole being–
In our legs and in our feet,
Enable us to walk the earth
With reverence and care;
So that we may walk in the ways of goodness and truth
And be protected from walking away from what is truth.

—Burnum Burnum, "Fire Blessing"

As a child growing up in Melbourne I never saw an Aboriginal person and knew little about Aboriginal history. In the mid-1970s I met Harry Penrith, who later changed his name to Burnum Burnum, after his great-grandfather. He gave regular talks about Aboriginal culture to my students and I became his most avid listener. Over the following decades I continued to learn more from Burnum Burnum and other Aboriginal elders.

In the 1990s I lived in New York. One Australia Day I sat next to Burnum Burnum by chance at a lecture! It was a great joy to catch up with our news and it was this day when Burnum Burnum gave me the gift of this prayer and permission to use it in my interfaith work.

The "Fire Blessing" is important to me because of its timeless wisdom and universal values. It is more than forty thousand years old and has been handed down through Aboriginal culture. The prayer shows us clearly the way to a transformed life when we are imbued with Fire and Spirit.

RABBI JACQUELINE TABICK

Rabbi Jacqueline Tabick was born in Dublin. She moved to London as a child and her family became involved in Reform Judaism. Ordained in 1975 by the Leo Baeck College in London, she was the first woman in the United Kingdom to become a rabbi. She is chair of the World Congress of Faiths, a patron of the Jewish Council for Racial Equality, and serves on the boards of the InterFaith Network and the Children of Abraham. She works in the North West Surrey Reform Synagogue (www.nwss.org.uk).

> Our God, and God of our ancestors, may it be Your will that the new moon come to us for goodness and blessing. May the new month bring us a life of fulfillment and peace, a life of goodness and blessing; a life of sustenance and health; a life filled with awe of God and fear of sin; a life without self-reproach and shame; a life of wealth and honor; a life marked by love of Your teaching and awe of God, when the desires of our hearts may be fulfilled for good. Amen.
>
> May [the New Moon] come to us and to all Israel for good.
>
> —"Prayer for the New Moon"

Judaism works on a combined lunar and solar calendar, so that while we change our months according to the phases of the moon, we can still observe harvest festivals in the correct season of the year. As each new moon approaches, heralding the beginning of the new month, we recite this prayer.

The prayer reminds me of a story that I read as a child of K'tonton, the Jewish version of Tom Thumb. K'tonton was a curious, bright child. One day, sitting in the synagogue, he heard the prayer for the new month and felt strongly that one of the phrases was unjustified. "Why," he wondered, "should our wishes and desires be limited to those which are 'for good'? Why cannot all our prayers and wishes be answered?" He then set to dreaming of his desire to see the world and, this being a story, there came a strong wind that lifted him into the air and set him off on a long journey, full of dangerous escapades, until he just longed for home and family.

Each month, this prayer calls me to do a reality check on my own life, reminding me to set my thoughts and dreams against the background of God's eternity. After all, I am just one finite being in God's great creation, full of other beings with equally important needs and desires. So what should be really important in my life? What should I pray for? What should I desire? What will contribute to the sum total of goodness in this wonderful world that God has allowed us to enjoy and how can I help with the ongoing process of bringing that to pass in this coming month?

DR. ELSA TAMEZ

Elsa was born in Mexico in 1950. At the age of eighteen she went to Costa Rica to study in the Latin America Biblical Seminary because women could not enroll in the Presbyterian Seminary in Mexico. Her theological studies within the context of the dictatorships and violence in Latin America led her to a faith commitment to the poor, women, and victims of violence. Elsa received her doctoral degree from the University of Lausanne, Switzerland. Her passion is reading the Bible from a liberating perspective, which helps to empower the marginalized. Author of several books including Jesus and Courageous Women, *Elsa lives in Costa Rica.*

The world is filled with pain, my God: so many innocent deaths, so much corruption everywhere, so many women assassinated.

As a woman, I feel impotent when seeing my sisters dominated and beaten. I ask myself, why were you not born among us as a woman? Maybe the situation would have changed a bit. We could then speak with dignity and without feeling inferior; we would walk with our heads held high like the gazelle; we would not be kept in silence or afraid to go outside alone, without being assaulted. Neither would we need to struggle against the churches' arguments that because Jesus was a man he only chose men to teach how to act in the world. But, maybe not, the structural sin of patriarchy is so strong that if you had been born as a woman, nobody would have believed you, like the disciples did not believe Mary Magdalena when she said that Jesus had risen from the dead. Or they could have manipulated your gender and message so that they would have served to legitimate the exclusion of women even more than now.

I feel ashamed to come to you, my God, because as humans we have not known how to be creatures that you could feel proud of. In my city there is no space to do good, to silence those who lie and are corrupt, to denounce the lack of justice and responsibility of transnational corporations. If I were to do that, they would call me a terrorist, ungrateful for the great favors and miracles of the free market. But what I see is the greed of the market and the financial world destroying equality, diversity, the planet and our sense of solidarity. How can we speak of your love and your grace in the midst of so much disgrace?

With your light I want to say NO MORE, as the prophets did, and call for indignation. I only ask for bravery and strength not to become paralyzed when confronted with a "wild" bullet of some hit man riding his motorcycle, hiding his face behind his helmet.

—Elsa Tamez

As a Christian, I feel great anxiety about the greed that is in Latin America and the world. Greed has generated violence, exploitation, and corruption that seem to be incurable. I always worry about the poor and women who are the first victims of this human degradation.

TSHERING TASHI

Tshering Tashi was born in Paro, Bhutan, where he spent much of his time on his mother's farm. After his education in India and Bhutan, he worked for the government of Bhutan for five years before resigning to serve as a militia officer in 2003 in the Low Intensity Conflict. Currently a businessman in Thimpu, Tshering is keen to ensure that Bhutan modernizes and does not Westernize. He is committed to Gross National Happiness (GNH), a concept originating in Bhutan. It attempts to measure quality of life and social progress in more holistic and psychological terms than Gross Domestic Product (GDP).

> As you are a son, parent, brother or a sibling?
> The members of the opposing forces are also
> someone to somebody. Buddhism does not
> allow you to kill, so how can you?
>
> —Yangbi Lopen

In 2003, Bhutan had to fight a war to flush out three groups of Indian militants from our soil. The fourth king led a small army on foot. Instead of bringing a general, he brought a senior monk who addressed the army of Bhutan before the battle. The war, described as a Low Intensity Conflict, lasted only two days but could have destroyed the nation state. Bhutan fought to win the trust and used it as a weapon to secure peace. Fighting to win battles is much easier.

ARCHBISHOP EMERITUS DESMOND TUTU

Desmond Tutu is Anglican archbishop emeritus of Cape Town, South Africa, and winner of the 1984 Nobel Peace Prize. After the fall of apartheid, Archbishop Tutu chaired the Truth and Reconciliation Commission. He is chair of The Elders, a group of senior world leaders dedicated to solving global problems and helping humanity, and he advocates worldwide for peace and forgiveness. His many books include No Future without Forgiveness, Made for Goodness: And Why This Makes All the Difference *(with daughter Rev. Mpho Tutu),* God is Not a Christian, *and* The Children of God Storybook Bible *(Desmond Tutu Peace Centre: www.tutu.org).*

Goodness is stronger than evil
Love is stronger than hate
Light is stronger than darkness
Life is stronger than death
Victory is ours through
Him who loves us.
Amen

—Desmond Tutu

I chose this prayer because it came to me at a time when we were being roughed up by the apartheid government, which seemed invincible. The prayer confirmed to us that victory was assured for goodness, etc. . . . It was a wonderful tonic at a dark time, this conviction that ours is indeed a moral universe.

REVEREND DR. OLAV FYKSE TVEIT

Norwegian born Reverend Dr. Olav Fykse Tveit is a Lutheran pastor who became general secretary of the World Council of Churches (WCC) in 2010. WCC is a Christian ecumenical organization seeking unity, a common witness and Christian service (www.oikoumene.org). Initially a parish priest and army chaplain, Olav later became involved in Norway's church affairs as general secretary for the Church of Norway Council on Ecumenical and International Relations. He was also a member of Norway's Interfaith Council and moderator of the Church of Norway's Islamic Council and Jewish Congregation contact groups.

O God, our help in ages past,
Our hope for years to come,
Our shelter from the stormy blast,
And our eternal home.

Under the shadow of Thy throne
Still may we dwell secure;
Sufficient is Thine arm alone,
And our defense is sure.

Before the hills in order stood,
Or earth received her frame,
From everlasting Thou art God,
To endless years the same.

Thy Word commands our flesh to dust,
Return, ye sons of men:
All nations rose from earth at first,
And turn to earth again.

A thousand ages in Thy sight
Are like an evening gone;
Short as the watch that ends the night
Before the rising sun.

The busy tribes of flesh and blood,
With all their lives and cares,
Are carried downwards by the flood,
And lost in following years.

Time, like an ever rolling stream,
Bears all its sons away;
They fly, forgotten, as a dream
Dies at the opening day.

Like flowery fields the nations stand
Pleased with the morning light;
The flowers beneath the mower's hand
Lie withering ere 'tis night.

O God, our help in ages past,
Our hope for years to come,
Be Thou our God while life shall last
And our eternal home.

Before the rising sun.

—Isaac Watts

This hymn, "O God, Our Help in Ages Past," is a prayer with many dimensions. It brings us into the cycle of years and ages passing by, but also to the eternal and present presence of God. The steadfastness of God's help, God's love and justice is what always remains—even when we do not see it. We pray to be able to see it, and we pray to God to make this a reality for all, forever! "Our hope for years to come, Be Thou our God while life shall last, And our eternal home."

MIRIAM-ROSE UNGUNMERR-BAUMANN, AM

Miriam-Rose Ungunmerr-Baumann is a well-known teacher, artist and writer with a passion for her Daly River community, Northern Territory, Australia. She was the territory's first fully qualified Aboriginal teacher and also worked there as an art consultant for many years. Her artworks, including Stations of the Cross, symbolize her deep love for both Christianity and Aboriginal spirituality. Miriam-Rose initiated a remote area teaching program, founded the Merrepen Arts Centre, and became principal of St. Francis Xavier School, Daly River. She has a Masters degree in education and was awarded an Order of Australia in 1998 for her services to Aboriginal education, art, and the community.

A special quality, a unique gift of Aboriginal people is *dadirri,*
which is inner, deep listening, and quiet, still awareness.

Dadirri recognizes the deep spring that is inside us. We call on it and it calls to us . . .
When I experience *dadirri,* I am made whole again. I can sit on the river bank or walk through the trees; even if someone close to me has passed away,
I can find my peace in this silent awareness.
There is no need for words.

Through the years we have listened to our stories.

They are told and sung, over and over, as the seasons go by.
The stories and songs sink quietly into our minds and we hold them deep inside.
In the ceremonies we celebrate the awareness of our lives as sacred...

In our Aboriginal way, we learnt to listen from our earliest days. We could not live good and useful lives unless we listened. We learnt by watching and listening, waiting and then acting.
Our people have passed on this way of listening for 40,000 years.
Quiet listening and stillness—*dadirri*—renews us and makes us whole.

My people are not threatened by silence. We are completely at home in it. We have lived for thousands of years with nature's quietness. My people recognize and experience in this quietness, the Great Life-Giving Spirit, the Father of us all.
When I am in the bush, among the trees, or by a billabong: these are the times I can simply be in God's presence. It is natural that we feel close to the Creator.

The other part of *dadirri* is the quiet stillness and the waiting.
Our Aboriginal culture has taught us to be still and to wait.
We do not try to hurry things up.
We let them follow their natural courses—like the seasons.

We watch the moon in each of its phases.
We wait for the rain to fill our rivers. And water
the thirsty earth.
We wait on God too. His time is the right time.
We wait for him to make his Word clear to us.

—Miriam-Rose Ungunmerr-Baumann

There are deep springs within each one of us. Within this deep spring, which is the very Spirit of God, is a sound. The sound of Deep calling to Deep. The sound is the Word of God—Jesus. Jesus enriches and renews our culture. He gently stirs our inner stillness but he does not take away our peace. We want to pass on the truth and goodness found in both our culture and traditions as well as in the gospels. The time for rebirth is now. If our culture is alive and strong and respected, it will grow. Our spirit will not die. And I believe that the spirit of *dadirri* that we have to offer will blossom and grow, not just within ourselves, but in our whole nation.

LILY VENIZELOS

Lily Venizelos is the founder and president of the Mediterranean Association to Save the Sea Turtles (MEDASSET), an international nongovernmental organization working for the study and conservation of sea turtles and their habitats throughout the Mediterranean (www.medasset.org). Since 1983, Lily has campaigned worldwide to raise awareness of the plight of the loggerhead sea turtles nesting in Laganas Bay, on the island of Zakynthos, Greece. The result was that the area was designated a national marine park in 1999. Among her many awards, Lily received one of the first Global 500 Awards from United Nations Environment Programme (UNEP) in 1987.

> Help me fly high without fear to make my dream come true: Strong belief in a dream is already a dream come true.
>
> —Lily Venizelos

My work with sea turtle conservation started as a dream. Twenty-eight years ago when I began believing in my dream, I knew little about the turtles and how to protect them. I took the plunge into ecology almost immediately and have never stopped since!

PROFESSOR DR. AMINA WADUD

Dr. Amina Wadud is professor emeritus of Islamic studies and is currently a visiting scholar at Starr King School for the Ministry in Berkeley, California. She has lived in five countries, including Egypt and Indonesia, and has traveled to more than forty countries as an international consultant on Islam, gender, justice and Qur'anic analysis. She is author of two books, Qur'an and Woman *and* Inside the Gender Jihad. *As a mother of five children, and now a grandmother, she focuses on feminist scholarship, Sufism, and activism for gender sensitive policy reforms as they relate to the lived realities of Muslim women.*

Allah/God does not place upon a soul/person
 more than it can bear.
To (each soul) is what it earns and against (each)
 is what it has accrued.
Our Lord:
Do not punish us, if we forget (are negligent), or
 if we err.
Our Lord:
Do not place a burden upon us like You placed
 upon others before us
Our Lord:
Do not place upon us what we cannot endure.
Pardon us

Forgive us
and have mercy upon us
You are our Lord

Help us against people who cover the truth (with falsehood).

—Qur'an 2:286

This Arabic passage taken from the Qur'an reads poetically: at the places where there is a cry for divine help, the language itself has the quality of a call, rendering the supplication twice as powerful in the original than in the English translation.

I like the way it describes the *nafs* (soul, person, or ego) as never having to endure anything more than it can bear or that it can achieve through its own effort, and yet, in the end, asking that we not have to endure more than we can bear. While this is a very personal and individual cry, the plural form indicates there is a collective human need for guidance in attaining truth, forgiveness, and mercy.

In its direct invocation to God there is a synchronicity between the everyday ordinary and the Sacred. Through God, we achieve the alleviation of our fears and the fulfillment of our needs.

YENNY WAHID

Yenny Wahid is a leading advocate and defender of Indonesia's long tradition of tolerance, compassion, and pluralism in its practice of Islam. A Harvard graduate and a former Sydney Morning Herald *and* The Age *journalist, she was part of a team that won the prestigious Walkley Award in 1999 for stories in Aceh and in post referendum Timor-Leste (East Timor). Yenny is currently director of the Wahid Institute, a non-profit organization founded by her father Abdurrahman Wahid to promote religious pluralism in Indonesia (www.wahidinstitute.org). Yenny is also involved in Indonesia's National Awakening Party.*

In the name of Allah, the beneficent, the merciful.
Praise be to the Lord of the Universe
who has created us and made us into tribes and nations,
That we may know each other, not that we may despise each other.
If the enemy incline towards peace,
do thou also incline towards peace,
and trust God, for the Lord is the one that
heareth and knoweth all things.
And the servants of God,
Most Gracious are those who walk on the Earth in humility,
and when we address them, we say "PEACE."

—Muslim prayer for peace

LECH WALESA

Lech Walesa co-founded Solidarność (Solidarity), the Soviet bloc's first independent trade union set up to secure workers' rights, including the right to strike and to organize independent unions. Lech was its first chairman. With his colleagues and co-workers he led the free non-communist unions gaining support from across the country. The movement, supported by the Catholic Church, led to the fall of communism in Poland. In January 1981 Lech met with Pope John Paul II in the Vatican. He was awarded the 1983 Nobel Peace Prize for his campaign for human rights and served as president of Poland from 1990 to 1995.

O God, you, who throughout long centuries,
have embraced Poland,
with your glory and power,
You, who have shielded her with your
loving care
and protected her from misfortunes
that were set to oppress her,

Refrain
At your altars we entreat you:
Bless our free Motherland, oh, Lord.

—Alojzy Feliński

For a long period of time we (Poland) had no independence, our land was "wasted," and we carried many burdens. Even now, this national hymn, *God Save Poland*, is known as a strong and forceful prayer for independence and peace. It is included in all Catholic Church hymn and prayer books and sung in many Polish churches, especially on national days.

In times of partition, occupation, and communism, the last line was sung as: "*Give us the Free Motherland, oh Lord.*"

DR. VAL WEBB

Val Webb, who is Australian born, has a career that spans microbiology, business, art, writing and theology. Her PhD is in religious studies. She has written nine books, her latest being Stepping Out with the Sacred: Human Attempts to Engage the Divine. *Her previous book,* Like Catching Water in a Net: Human Attempts to Describe the Divine, *won the Best Books USA 2007 Award for general religion (www.valwebb.com.au).*

> To wonder is to perceive with reverence and love... and in wondering we come close to the feeling that the earth is holy. Historically, the notion of wonder has been closely bound up with a religious mode of being in the world. Perhaps a century ago the chapel would have been an appropriate background, but now things seem to have changed... In my experience, the substance of wonder is more frequently found in the prose of the secular than in the often quaint poetry of religion. The sacred is in the profane... the wonder is in the world...
>
> Whether we continue to talk about God is not so important as whether we retain the sense of wonder which keeps us aware that ours is a holy place.
>
> —Sam Keen

We live in a very different world today. In our global village, one faith tradition can no longer make exclusive claims about God, condemning all others to judgment. Religion can no longer set itself up against science, claiming absolute truth against our increasing knowledge of the universe. A Divine Being outside the world orchestrating events to favor some and not others and interfering with natural laws no longer makes sense for many. Humans cannot continue to violate the earth by claiming a religious mandate to subdue it.

All these changes have challenged God-talk, such that progressive religious thinkers are now recovering ancient metaphors and images from across religions, metaphors and images of the Sacred within the universe—whether called Energy, Presence, Love, Spirit, Ground of Being, Life, or else the world as the Divine Body.

This imagining of the Sacred as an integral part of the universe, not outside it and organizing its events, allows us to talk with science about the wondrous organism we share and the mystery we all seek to unravel and experience, whether described in religious, natural or scientific terms.

It also demands that we treat our world with respect, including all its creatures, its elements and its laws for survival. In this scenario, human wonder becomes prayer, not as a shopping list of requests to an elsewhere God, but as experiencing the Divine within or sinking deep into the Divine Life. Simply to live is to experience the holiness of life.

DR. DEBORAH WEISSMAN

Deborah Weissman, who was born in New York, settled in Jerusalem in 1972. She currently teaches at four Christian institutions in Jerusalem and has received many awards for her Jewish educational work in Israel. She is co-chair of the Inter-Religious Coordinating Council in Israel and the first Jewish woman to be elected president of the International Council of Christians and Jews in the council's sixty year history (www.iccj.org). Deborah is a religious feminist who works for peace through dialogue.

> ...For according to Your name so is Your praise. You are slow to anger and ever ready to be reconciled; for you desire not the death of the sinner, but that he repent and live. And even until the day of his death You await him; and if he returns, You straightaway receive him.
>
> In truth, You are their Creator, who knows their nature, that they are flesh and blood. As for a human, she is from the dust and unto the dust will she return; she gets her bread with the peril of her life, she is like a fragile shard, withering grass, a fading flower, a fleeting shadow, a passing cloud, the blowing wind, the floating dust, a transient dream.
>
> But You are the King, the living and everlasting God.
>
> —Extract from *Unetaneh Tokef*,
a traditional Jewish prayer
from the Middle Ages

The *Unetaneh Tokef* is a liturgical poem from the Middle Ages that has become a traditional Jewish prayer recited on Yom Kippur, the Day of Atonement, by Jews of every denomination and ethnic background. Ashkenazi Jews with a European heritage also recite it on Rosh Hashanah, the Jewish New Year.

Our sages taught that there are two traditions regarding the day the world was created. One is that heaven and earth were created on Rosh Hashanah, the first day of the Hebrew month of Tishrei. But an alternate tradition maintains that heaven and earth were created six days earlier, on the twenty-fifth of Elul, and that the first of Tishrei actually celebrates the creation of Adam, the first human being.

Taken together, the two traditions thus set up a parallel between one human being and the whole world, and, indeed, the *Mishnah* (the first layer of the Talmud [Oral Law] compiled by Rabbis in the land of Israel) teaches that whoever saves the life of one human being has saved a whole world, while whoever—God forbid—kills one human being has destroyed an entire world.

May we all recognize the preciousness and precariousness of every human life. The creation text also indicates that all human beings, both male and female, were created in the Divine Image. May we strive to ensure that all people are granted the dignity and equal rights that are their due.

CLAUDETTE ANTOINE WERLEIGH

Claudette Werleigh was the first female prime minister of Haiti and was also secretary-general of Pax Christi International, a global Catholic peace movement working for human rights and a just world order. She has also worked for Caritas and the Life and Peace Institute. Claudette is a registered lawyer and her working experience in nonformal adult education has been strongly influenced by Paolo Freire's empowerment approach. Another influence is liberation theology with its preference for the poor and the most marginalized in society. Her main areas of interest are advocacy, community development, environment, human rights, and empowering women (http://www.windowsonhaiti.com).

> O Lord! O my Dear God!
> Such a strong rain!
> It is washing away several days, weeks and even months of very hard labor.
> Nevertheless, I give you thanks, my dear God,
> Because this rain that is causing me so much trouble,
> Perhaps is bringing joy and happiness to other people.
>
> —Prayer by a poor Haitian farmer

The poor peasant who said this prayer did not know that I was listening. He was talking to his God!

I was participating in a summer school camp in Chatard, a mountainous region in the northern part of Haiti.

While we were heading back to the camp one late afternoon, the temperature suddenly dropped and it started to rain heavily. Together with a classmate, I took refuge under the thatched roof of a poor farmer's hut. As soon as he saw us, the farmer hurried to prepare some hot coffee to keep us warm. While he was busy setting up the fire, I heard the famer talk and I wondered who it was he was talking to. Totally unaware that I was paying full attention, I heard him relate the devastating effects of the rain that was washing away days and weeks, perhaps even months of his work. And he concluded by saying: "But I give you thanks, my dear God, because this rain that is causing me so much trouble, perhaps is bringing joy and happiness to other people."

This poor peasant was able to go beyond his own situation and reach out to other people whom he could not even see. It revealed a deep sense of humanity and gives the word fraternity (brotherhood/sisterhood) its full meaning.

ARCHBISHOP ROWAN WILLIAMS

Rowan Williams has been archbishop of Canterbury since 2002. He was born in 1950 and brought up in Swansea, Wales. From 1986 to 1992 he was Lady Margaret Professor of Divinity at Oxford. He served as bishop of Monmouth from 1992 and Archbishop of Wales from 2000. Dr. Williams is a fellow of the British Academy and is the author of several books on theology. He is married to Jane, a writer and teacher; they have two children.

Sun, who all my life dost brighten,
Light, who dost my soul enlighten,
Joy, the sweetest man e'er knoweth,
Fount whence all my being floweth;
At thy feet I cry, my maker,
Let me be a fit partaker
Of this blessed food from heaven,
For our good, thy glory, given.

Jesus, Bread of Life, I pray thee,
Let me gladly here obey thee.
Never to my hurt invited,
Be thy love with love requited.
From this banquet let me measure,
Lord, how vast and deep its treasure;
By the gifts thou here dost give me
As thy guest in heaven receive me.

—Johann Franck, "*Schmücke dich o liebe Seele*"

I suppose these words are the ones I most frequently repeat in prayer—apart from the Lord's Prayer itself and the fixed forms of prayer I use every day as a priest. For as long as I can remember, I've used them as a prayer after Holy Communion, and since I'll be at Communion nearly every day, they are very much part of my life. The hymn of which they form a part is an old German Lutheran one, but the vision expressed is one that practically any Christian could make their own. The words speak of the extraordinary fact that the God who is the source of all things has invited us to sit down at the table with his Son, to be a part of his "household," and to receive something of his eternal and unimaginable joy. We know we don't and can't deserve to be there, but we pray that we may somehow be made worthy to share in this. God gives us this gift so that we may grow and rejoice more deeply, and also to show his own radiant beauty, the brightness and splendor of unconditional love; it's for his glory as well as our good.

We receive this love and we pray that we become able to return it—toward God and toward each other. And as this happens, we come that bit closer to our proper destiny. To be God's guest here at the Lord's table is to experience the first beginnings of being God's guest in heaven. And as we look around, we see all those who are sharing with us in Communion as likewise God's guests—so that we see how we have to welcome them all as well, since if God wants their company, we are not in a very good position to object!

Holy Communion means many different things to Christians; but for the majority of them, it's the moment when our own prayers are most fully taken up into the prayer of Jesus to his Father. When we receive the bread and wine as his body and blood, his active presence, we come to stand where he stands and speak with his words. All Christian prayer has this character, but in the Eucharist it is most clearly set out. This is where we receive in fullest form that love which is the "fount" from which all our life derives; and in us—to borrow an image from Charles Wesley—the fount rises up in our hearts, and God's love kindled to life in us responds to God's love coming to us. And that's what prayer is all about, I believe.

RABBI JONATHAN WITTENBERG

Scottish born Jonathan Wittenberg has German Jewish roots with rabbinic ancestors on both sides. After reading English at Cambridge, he trained for the rabbinate and was ordained in 1987. He is currently rabbi of the New North London Synagogue and senior rabbi of the Assembly of Masorti Synagogues UK (www.masorti.org.uk). With a keen interest in pastoral care, particularly for the sick and dying, as well as Jewish/Christian and Jewish/Muslim interfaith dialogue, Jonathan has initiated a project to create a multi-faith secondary school. He is an enthusiastic walker and author of many books including The Silence of Dark Water: An Inner Journey.

Hear our voice, O Lord our God, have mercy on
us and pity us; accept our prayer with favor
and with love.

Bring us back to you, God, and we shall return;
renew our days as of old.

Do not cast us away from you; do not take your
sacred spirit from us.

Do not cast us off in our old age; when our
strength grows weak do not forsake us.

—The *Shema Koleinu*

These tender verses are sung to an unforgettable melody at key moments during the Day of Atonement, the most sacred date in the Jewish year. In the synagogue the holy Ark is opened to reveal the Torah scrolls and the congregation stands. I shall never forget seeing my aged father, barely able to attend services any longer, weeping at the poignant beauty of these words.

This prayer is a call from heart to heart, from the heart of the human being, any and every human being, to the heart of God, seeking only acceptance and love.

In asking God not to take the sacred spirit from us, the prayer affirms that the essence of being human is to know that our spirit, vitality, and creativity come from God and that life is a brief but immense privilege.

The prayer addresses God out of a deep awareness of our vulnerability. In illness and old age, stages of life so often scorned in the utilitarian ethos of contemporary society, we ask God to be with us and so give us inner strength and insight.

For all those reasons I love these words and find them humbling. The music to which they are sung renders them sublime.

PASTOR DR. JAMES MOVEL WUYE

Pastor James Movel Wuye is a Christian Evangelist. With Imam Ashafa, he is co-founder and co-director of the Interfaith Mediation Centre in Kaduna, Nigeria, a faith-based peace-building organization. Founded in 1995 by two former bitter religious enemies: Pastor James Wyue and Imam Ashafa (see page 17), the Centre is responsible for mediating peace between Christians and Muslims (www.imc-nigeria.org). Their story is one of triumph and transformation, from hate to love, from vengeance to forgiveness, and from exclusion to inclusion. The story has been made into the film, The Imam and the Pastor.

I know there is but One Mind, which is the Mind of God, in which all people live and move and have their being.

I know there is a Divine Pattern for humanity and within this pattern there is infinite harmony and peace, cooperation, unity and mutual helpfulness.

I know that the mind of humankind, being one with the Mind of God, shall discover the method, the way and the means best fitted to permit the flow of Divine Love between individuals and nations.

I know there shall be a free interchange of ideas, of cultures, of spiritual concepts, of ethics, of

educational systems and scientific discoveries–
for all good belongs to all alike.

I know that because the Divine Mind has created
us all, we are bound together in one infinite and
perfect unity.

In bringing about World Peace, I know that all
people and all nations will remain individual but
unified for the common purpose of promoting
peace, happiness, harmony, and prosperity.

I know that deep within each person the Divine
Pattern of perfect peace is already implanted.

I now declare that in each person and in leaders
of thought everywhere this Divine Pattern moves
into action and form, to the end that all nations
and all people shall live together in peace,
harmony and prosperity forever.

So it is now.

–Ernest Holmes, *A Prayer for World Peace*

I believe this is God's purpose for mankind.

XINRAN

Born in Beijing in 1958, Xinran was a journalist and radio presenter in China. In 1997 she moved to London, where she wrote her best-selling book about Chinese women's lives, The Good Women of China. *Xinran writes regularly for* The Guardian *newspaper and appears frequently on radio and TV. Her other books include* Sky Burial *and* Message from an Unknown Chinese Mother, *which is about Chinese mothers who have lost their daughters. Xinran is founder of The Mothers' Bridge of Love, which acts as a bridge of understanding between Chinese adoptive culture and birth culture (www.mothersbridge.org).*

Beloved Child
Do you see me in your dreams?
Every day I wait for you . . .
I wait
For the wind to bring me your breath
For the light to bring me your colours
I pray
The daytime makes you smile
The night-time brings you peace

Beloved Child
If the rain touches you, it is my tears
If the wind caresses you, it is my hand
The daylight is my watching eye over you
The night-time is my cradling of your dreams.

Beloved Child
Do you see me in your dreams?

Every door that opens is my arms embracing you
Thank you
My daughter
Thank you
For being my unforgotten daughter.

—Xinran

I wrote this poem for a little girl called Little Snow whom I fostered but, due to Chinese social and political mores at the time, was forced to give her up. I was heartbroken but gained some understanding of how hard it is for mothers to give up their children, usually girls. As well as giving them the gift of life, their love stays forever and their daughters are constantly in their thoughts and dreams.

Many, but not all, adopted Chinese girls are aware that their birth mothers challenged social conventions. These mothers often suffered oppression and ignorance, costing them years of hardship, anguish, and sacrifice in order for their daughters to be alive and thriving today.

DR. SAKENA YACOOBI

Dr. Sakena Yacoobi is a social activist who is passionate about Afghanistan and education. She founded the Afghan Institute of Learning (AIL) in 1995 to improve the health and education of Afghan women and children (www.afghaninstituteoflearning.org). Since the fall of the Taliban in 2001, the institute has provided a range of complementary health and education programs for women and children. These include Women's Learning Centers, which offer education from preschool to university level, health instruction, and income-generating skills. Recognized as one of the principal educators in Afghanistan today, Sakena Yacoobi has received many awards including the 2004 Gruber Prize for Women's Rights and the 2007 Gleitsman International Activist Award.

Bismillah al rahman al rahim
*(In the name of God,
most Gracious,
most Compassionate)*

—Qur'an

For me, this Arabic phrase is the very essence of Islam and also the very essence of who I am. I say this phrase when I awake in the morning and before I go to sleep at night. Before every journey, before any act that I take, I say this phrase. It is always on my lips and always in my heart. When I say this, I feel a direct connection to God and I feel protected, peaceful and secure, knowing that I am in God's protection and God will guide my actions and my words and my very being.

All chapters of the Qur'an, except one, begin with these words. It is a very hard phrase to translate. The common English translation is *In the name of God, most Gracious, most Compassionate* but, for me, these words fail to capture the true depth of meaning or its full inspirational message. Here are several poetic interpretations I like:

> With every breath that we breathe, may we act on behalf of the Divine Presence, the Source of all that we receive.
>
> With every step that we take, may we be instruments of the One Light which guides us, the Source and Nourisher of all of creation.
>
> Every moment of this life is filled with your eternal radiance my Beloved, You are the Beneficent One who endlessly showers all of creation with nourishment and blessings, and the One who generously rewards those who live in harmony with Your Divine Will.
>
> —www.wahiduddin.net

HAMZA YUSUF

Hamza Yusuf was born in the United States. His father was a Scots Irish Catholic and his mother half-Irish and Greek. Raised in the Greek Orthodox tradition, Hamza Yusuf adopted Islam at eighteen after studying the world's major religions. For ten years, he studied Islamic sciences in the Middle East before returning to the United States to teach and write. Co-founder of Zaytuna Institute, an Islamic school devoted to classical scholarship, he currently works at Zaytuna College, the first accredited Muslim college in the United States (www.zaytuna.org). He is the author of many books, including Purification of the Heart, *and lives in California with his family.*

> O God, show me truth as truth and enable me
> to adhere to it; and show me falsehood as
> falsehood and enable me to avoid it.
>
> —Prophet Muhammad

This prayer is an extraordinary testimony to the humility of the Prophet Muhammad as well as his keen understanding of human nature. Delusion is a common affliction of humanity. Most of us are deluded about something, if not many things, especially our own state. It is often easy to see the faults of others or to recognize when they have gone wrong, but it is much harder to see our own faults. The truth can be in plain sight of someone and yet that person may be entirely incapable of seeing it as truth. Or they might recognize it as truth but find themselves incapable of following it.

Likewise, falsehood often presents itself embellished in truth. False prophets succeed by dressing lies in truth. Sometimes we see falsehood but are seduced by it and unable to avoid it. This prayer covers all of that in its profound simplicity.

In another prayer, from the Al-Bukhari Collection of hadith or prophetic traditions, the Prophet said, "*O God, show me things as they really are.*" The duality of appearance and reality is a great motif in literature. We often mistake one for the other. This prayer reminds us that we need providential care to protect us from our delusions. Humility is a great religious virtue and too often absent among religious people.

ST. ETHELBURGA'S CENTRE FOR RECONCILIATION AND PEACE, LONDON, UK

St. Ethelburga's Centre for Reconciliation and Peace has arisen from the ruins of St. Ethelburga's Church, after its destruction by an Irish Republican Army bomb in 1993. The Centre is now an independent charity that aims to encourage and enable people to practice reconciliation and peace-making in their communities and lives.

Since the Centre opened in 2003, well over 50,000 people from forty-one countries and many places of conflict have visited the Centre to share stories, experiences, insights and skills about how people can build relationships across divisions of conflict and religion.

For many, St Ethelburga's is a powerful symbol of how the chaos of conflict can be transformed into a new creative order. Their experience and ideas come from listening to these people, rather than from any particular theoretical or theological position. The Centre also has a unique (Bedouin) Tent that offers a safe and sacred space for people of different faiths to explore together how to understand their differences, transform conflicts, and develop shared values and strategies for collaboration in a changing world.

London is one of the most cosmopolitan cities in the world and, some say, in history. We therefore share a powerful responsibility to demonstrate to the world how people of vastly different backgrounds, cultures, religions and worldviews can share the city's crowded space and live together peacefully.

www.stethelburgas.org

INFORMATION ON SOURCES

Page 1

Rabindranath Tagore (1861–1941) was an Indian poet. This poem, "Where the mind is without fear," is from *Gitanjali*, a collection of 103 inspirational poems.

Page 3

This quotation is adapted from *Tao Te Ching*, verse 25, final 4 lines, as translated by Chungliang Al Huang. The *Tao Te Ching* (The Way of Life) was written approximately 2,500 years ago and is regarded as a classic Chinese text embracing the fundamentals of Taoism. Laozi, a mystic philosopher of ancient China, is traditionally considered to be the author of *Tao Te Ching* but this is still under debate.

Page 5

St. Teresa of Avila (1515–1582) was a Carmelite nun and a Spanish mystic. She suffered severe illness when young and through this discovered the power of prayer. Over the years, she founded seventeen reformed Carmelite houses. Canonized in 1622, St. Teresa was made a Doctor of the Church in 1970. She is the patron saint of sick people, lace makers, opposition to church authorities, people in need of grace, people in religious orders, and Spain. The quotation here, translated by James Alison, is an excerpt from *Santa Teresa de Jesús, Obras completas* (Biblioteca de Autores Cristianos, Madrid 1997), 667–68.

Page 7

Brother Roger Schutz (1915–2005) was a Swiss Protestant who founded the Taizé ecumenical community in 1940. Famous for its worship, liturgy, Bible study, and chants, Taizé welcomes people of all ages, especially young adults. The community encourages people to take the message of Taizé back to their own countries and to be creators of trust and reconciliation. The lines quoted here are from Brother Roger of Taizé's *A Life We Never Dared Hope For* (Oxford:

Mowbray Books, 1980), 36–37. *A life we never dared hope for, Brother Roger of Taizé* © Ateliers et Presses de Taizé, 71250 Taizé Community, France.

Page 9
The selection here, Surah Al-Ahqaf (The Wind-Curved Sandhills), is from Dr. Ahmad Zaki Hammad, *The Gracious Qur'an: A Modern-Phrased Interpretation in English,* Surah 46:15 (Lucent Interpretations, 2008), 879.

Page 11
This selection from 1 Corinthians is taken from two translations: 1 Corinthians 13:8–10 is from *The Holy Bible, New International Version,* and 1 Corinthians 13:11–13; 14:1 is from *The Holy Bible, New Revised Standard Version.*

Page 13
Fethullah Gülen (1941–) is a Muslim scholar, intellectual and a poet. (See page 68 for his contribution.) This poem is taken from M. Syafi'i Anwar, "Ketika Pluralisme Diharamkan dan Kebebasan Beragama Dicederai: Sebuah Kaleidoskop, Pengalaman, dan Kesaksian untuk Mas Djohan Effendi," ["When pluralism was categorised as haram (forbidden) and the freedom of religon was restricted: a kaledioscope and witness to human experience for Mas Djohan Effendi"] in *Merayakan Kebebasan Beragama: Bunga Rampai Menyambut 70 tahun Djohan Effendi,* [Celebrating the Freedom of Religion: an anthology of 70 years of Effendi], Djohan Effendi, Abd. Moqsith Ghazali, (Penerbit Buku Kompas, 2009), 463.

Page 15
The selection here, Surah Al-Ahzab (The Coalition), is from the Qur'an translated by Abdullah Yusuf Ali in 1934.

Page 17
Movement for Reforming Society, Main Canal Road, Near Fatehgarh Bridge, Moghalpura, Lahore-54840, Pakistan.

Page 21
Marian Wright Edelman (1939–) is an American activist for children's rights. This prayer is from her book, *Guide My Feet: Prayers and Meditations on Loving and Working for Children* (Boston: Bea-

con Press, 1995), 88. Copyright © 1995 by Marian Wright Edelman Reprinted by permission of Beacon Press, Boston.

Page 25
D. H. Lawrence (1885–1930) was an English novelist, poet, playwright, essayist, literary critic and painter. *Lady Chatterley's Lover* was his most famous and controversial novel. Between 1926 and 1928 Lawrence wrote the final version three times. He first wrote *A Propos of "Lady Chatterley's Lover"* as an introduction to the second edition under the title *My Skirmish with Jolly Roger*; it was later revised and published posthumously in 1930. It is a defense, explanation, and history of the novel. The excerpt here is from D. H. Lawrence, *A Propos of "Lady Chatterley's Lover"* (London: Penguin Books, 1994), 323, 329. Copyright © the Estate of Frieda Lawrence Ravagli 1993. Cambridge edition of *A Propos of "Lady Chatterley's Lover,"* David Herbert Lawrence, 1993. Reproduced by permission of Pollinger Limited and The Estate of Frieda Lawrence Ravagli.

Page 27
The "O Antiphons" are seven short verses recited (or chanted) before the Magnificat during Evening Prayer of the Christian Church on the seven days before the vigil of Christmas. Their exact origin is unknown but it is likely that they were first composed in the seventh or eighth century when monks put together texts from the Old Testament that expressed the Christian Church's yearning for the long expected Savior.

Page 30
The *Vedas* are the primary texts of Hinduism. Rigveda is the first of four main texts. This selection is from Pandit Satyakam Vidyalankared, *The Holy Vedas: A Golden Treasury* (Delhi: Clarion Books, 2010), epigraph. Reproduced with permission.

Page 32
Leonardo Boff, "Prayer to the Mother Earth and Sacrament of God," in *A opção Terra: a solução para a Terra não cai do céu*, Record, Rio de Janeiro 2009, 219, translated by Jenna Tregarthen. Used with permission.

Page 34
This excerpt from Psalm 23 is taken from *The Holy Bible, King James Version.* The Kokoda Track is a single-file path that runs ninety-six kilometers through the Owen Stanley Range in Papua New Guinea.

It is the renowned location of the World War II battle between Japanese and Australian forces in 1942 and crosses some of the most rugged and isolated terrain in the world.

Page 35
"May the Spirit" by Rev. Dr. Marcus Braybrooke. Passage written for this compilation. Used with permission. © Marcus Braybrooke.

Page 37
Ernesto Cardenal, "Hear My Cries: Psalm 5," *Psalms*, Crossroad Publishing, 1981, translated by John Griffiths. Reproduced by kind permission of Continuum International Publishing Group.

Page 39
John Harriott (1933–1990) was a former Jesuit priest, a journalist, and a broadcaster. These lines are extracted from "Our World," in *Fields of Praise: The Glory of Being Human* (Great Wakering, UK: Mayhew-McCrimmon, 1976), 19. *Fields of Praise* © 1976 McCrimmon Publishing Co Ltd, Great Wakering, Essex, England.

Page 41
This excerpt is from *The New Jerusalem Bible*.

Page 43
John McConnell (1951–) teaches spirituality and Buddhist psychology as a practical resource in handling difficult life-situations, particularly conflict and ill-health. He has been a student of the Dhamma for nearly forty years, and is a member of the Religious Society of Friends. This excerpt is from his book, *Healing Anxiety Through Meditation—A Buddhist Approach* (Sri Lanka: Buddhist Cultural Centre, 2007), 206–14.

Page 45
Sr. Mary Lou Kownacki, OSB (1941–) is the coordinator of Monasteries of the Heart (www.monasteriesoftheheart.org). This "Prayer for Dialogue with Greater Religions" is in her *Prayers for a New Millennium* (Missouri: Liguori Publications, 1998), 24. Used with permission.

Page 47
Shantideva was an eighth-century Buddhist sage. His famous *Bodhicharyavatara* is regarded as the quintessential Buddhist text on compassion and has been a constant source of inspiration for the

great masters of Tibet. The selection quoted here is from *A Guide to the Bodhisattva's Way of Life,* chapter 5, verses 12–14, translated by Stephen Batchelor, Library of Tibetan Works and Archives.

Page 49
John Henry Cardinal Newman (1801–1890) was an Oxford academic and Anglican clergyman who converted to Catholicism in 1845. He was made a cardinal in 1870 by Pope Leo XIII, and was beatified by Pope Benedict XVI in September 2010. This prayer, entitled "Radiating Christ," was chosen by Mother Teresa of Calcutta to be recited by the Missionaries of Charity every morning after Holy Mass.

Page 51
All Central Asian monks and nuns know the *King of Mahayana Prayers* by heart. It is found in a large compendium sutra known as *The Avatamsaka,* a work considered by most Mahayana Buddhists to be the most transcendental of all the discourses of the Buddha, and also to be the discourse creating the bridge to Buddha's tantric teachings. The excerpt presented here, "The Great King of Prayers" from the Avatamsaka Sutra, is taken from *The King of Mahayana Aspirations* (Skt. *Mahayana-pranidana-raja),* otherwise known as *The Samantabhadra Prayer* (Skt. *Samantabhadra-pranidana),* translated into English in the twentieth century by Glenn H. Mullin with Thepo Tulku, in accordance with a commentary by the second-century Indian master Nagarjuna.

Page 53
The full version of the article on this prayer by Fr. Paolo Dall'Oglio is available at http://www.deirmarmusa.org/node/189.

Page 55
This passage, entitled "Desert," was written by Mariama De Lys Walet Mohamed for this compilation.

Page 57
These verses are from *The New American Bible.*

Page 61
Martha Postlethwaite (1956–) is an associate professor of spiritual formation, spiritual director, chaplain, and ordained elder in the

United Methodist Church of the United States. The poem "Clearing" is used with permission.

Page 63
Fr. John Main (1926–1982) rediscovered and revived the practice of meditation in the Christian tradition. This prayer is from John Main, OSB, *The Essential Teaching* (Audio), CD#1, Track 1 (1993). Used with permission of Medio Media.

Page 64
The *Shema* is an affirmation of Judaism and a declaration of faith in one God. Jesus quotes part of the Shema (Dt 6:4–5) in Mark 12:29–30. Martin Buber (1878–1965) was an Austrian born Jewish philosopher and theologian. Martin Buber, *I and Thou,* trans. Walter Kaufmann (New York: Scribner, 1970), 182. Reprinted with the permission of Scribner, a Division of Simon & Schuster, Inc., from I AND THOU by Martin Buber. Copyright © 1970 by Charles Scribner's Sons. All rights reserved and also by kind permission of Continuum International Publishing Group.

Page 66
The selection here, from Surah Al Nisa (Women), is from the Qur'an translated by M. A. S. Abdel Haleem in 2004.

Page 68
This prayer, written by Fethullah Gülen for this compilation, was translated by Zuleyha Keskin. Passages from the Qur'an in the reflection are from the Qur'an translated by Abdullah Yusuf Ali in 1934.

Page 70
Taoism is a Chinese philosophy and religion that seeks harmony and long life through the philosophy of simplicity and non-interference with the natural course of things.

Page 71
This prayer is an excerpt from Shantideva's *Bodhicharyavatara,* Chapter X, Dedication. Shantideva was an eighth-century Indian master and scholar. His famous *Bodhicharyavatara* is regarded as the quintessential Buddhist text on compassion and has been a constant source of inspiration for the great masters of Tibet.

Page 72
This selection from Ephesians is taken from *Life, Application Study Bible,* New King James Version (Illinois: Tyndale House Publishers Inc., 1997), 2162. New King James Version®. Copyright © 1982 by Thomas Nelson, Inc. Used by permission. All rights reserved.

Page 74
William Edward Burghardt Du Bois (1868-1963) was an American civil-rights leader and author. These two prayers, "Micah 6:1–8" and "Esther 4:9–16," are reprinted from his *Prayers for Dark People,* by W. E. B. Du Bois, ed. Herbert Aptheker (Amherst: University of Massachusetts Press, 1980) 29, 21. Copyright © 1980 by the University of Massachusetts Press and published by the University of Massachusetts Press.

Page 76
Yehuda Amichai (1924–2000) was one of Israel's most celebrated poets. This poem, "The place where we are right," is taken from *The Selected Poetry of Yehuda Amichai,* edited and translated by Chana Bloch and Stephen Mitchell (London: University of California Press, 1996), 34. © 1996 by Chana Bloch and Stephen Mitchell. Published by the University of California Press.

Page 78
Nichiren (1222–1282) was a Japanese Buddhist monk and teacher. This selection is taken from *Nichiren Daishonin Gosho Zenshu* (The Collected Writings of Nichiren Daishonin) (The Soka Gakkai, 1952), 784. Used with permission of Soka Gokkai.

Page 80
The selection here, Surah Al-Baqarah (The Cow), is from the Qur'an translated by Yusuf Ali in 1934.

Page 83
This poem, entitled "Religion" is from *Companion of God, The Wisdom and Words of Dadi Janki* published by Brahma Kumaris Services Ltd., Publications Division. For further details visit www.bkpublications.com.

Page 85
These words from Monica Jeddah Otto were written for this compilation.

Page 87
Mawlana Shaykh Nazim Adil Al-Haqqani (1922–) is Grand Shaykh of the Tariqa and leader of the Naqshbandi-Haqqani Sufi Order.

Page 89
Sri Guru Gobind Singh Ji (1666–1708) was the tenth master or guru of the Sikh faith. This prayer is the epilogue to *Chandi Charitar, Sri Dasam Granth—The Holy Scripture of Khalsa*, 231.

Page 91
Franz Jägerstätter (1907–1943) was beatified in Linz Cathedral, Austria, in 2007. This selection is from *Franz Jägerstätter: A Different Kind of Hero* (Pax Christi, 2008). Used with permission.

Page 93
Profits from *A World of Prayer* will go to St. Ethelburga's Centre for Reconciliation and Peace. For more information about this organization, please see page 212.

Page 95
This selection from Azim Khamisa is used with permission.

Page 97
This selection from the Qur'an, Al-Raad (The Thunder), is from the Sahih International translation.

Page 99
The selection here, Al-Fatihah (The Opening), was translated by Halima Krausen. Al-Fatihah is the first Surah of the Qur'an and consists of seven verses. It has an essential role in Muslim prayers and is repeatedly recited in daily worship.

Page 101
Kautilya Chanakaya (c. 350–283 BCE) was an Indian politician, economist, and writer known for his wisdom and knowledge.

Page 102
Peggy Ann Way (1931–) is an ordained minister in the United Church of Christ. This selection is from her book, *Women's Liberation and the Church* (New York: Association Press in cooperation with IDOC-North America, 1970), 90.

Page 104
This selection is from Hans Küng's book *Islam: Past Present and Future*, translated by John Bowden (Oxford: Oneworld Publications, 2007), 642. Used with permission.

Page 106
Kyong Ho (1849–1912) was a famous Korean Zen master who was key to reviving modern Korean Zen Buddhism. This selection from Kyong Ho is taken from Mu Soeng, *Thousand Peaks: Korean Zen Tradition and Teachers* (California: Parallax Press, 1987), 162, and used with Mu Soeng's permission.

Page 108
Rainer Maria Rilke (1875–1926) was a Bohemian-Austrian poet and art critic and is considered one of the greatest lyric poets of modern Germany. This sonnet is from Rilke's Sonnets to Orpheus, Part 2, 29, and is the December 1 reading ""Let This Darkness Be a Bell Tower" from A YEAR WITH RILKE, TRANSLATED AND EDITED by JOANNA MACY and ANITA BARROWS. Copyright © 2009 by Joanna Macy and Anita Barrows. Reprinted by permission of HarperCollins Publishers.

Page 110
St. Francis of Assisi (1181–1226) is one of the most celebrated and best-loved saints, remembered for his gentleness and his willingness to see God's presence in all aspects of nature. He is known as the patron saint of ecologists, animals, Assisi, and Italy. The peace prayer printed here is associated with St. Francis, as it is often published on a card with his portrait. Research shows, however, that it was written in 1912 in France by a priest and widely circulated during World War I.

Page 112
William Henley (1849–1903) was an English poet, critic, and editor. The piece printed here, "Invictus," is his most famous poem. It was written in 1875, most likely to demonstrate Henley's resilience following the amputation of his foot after it became infected with tuberculosis. Nelson Mandela's reflection is a quote from the Nelson Mandela Centre of Memory, Nelson Mandela Foundation.

Page 114
T. S. Eliot (1888–1965) was an American-born poet, playwright, and literary critic who received the 1948 Nobel Prize in literature.

The passage quoted here is an excerpt from "Little Gidding," the final poem of T. S. Eliot's *Four Quartets*, a series of poems that discuss time, perspective, humanity, and the divine. Little Gidding refers to a village in Huntingdonshire (now part of Cambridgeshire, UK), visited by Eliot in 1936. Excerpt from "Little Gidding" from FOUR QUARTETS copyright 1942 by T. S. Eliot and renewed 1970 by Esme Valerie Eliot, reprinted by permission of Houghton Mifflin Harcourt Publishing Company and Faber and Faber Ltd.

Page 116
Mohandas Karamchand Gandhi (1869–1948) was an Indian political and spiritual leader. This is an adaptation of Gandhi's original words, which read, "I do not want my house to be walled in on all sides and my windows to be stifled. I want the cultures of all the lands to be blown about my house as freely as possible. But I refuse to be blown off my feet by any."

Page 117
E. F. Schumacher (1911–1977) was an influential thinker on alternative economics, philosophy, and "appropriate technology." This selection is from his book, *Good Work* (New York: Harper & Row, 1979), 34–35. Excerpt from GOOD WORK by E. F. Schumacher. Copyright © 1979 by Verena Schumacher. Reprinted by permission of HarperCollins Publishers.

Page 121
This selection from the Qur'an is from Surah A'sr (The Declining Day), translation by Abdulluh Yusuf Ali, New Edition.

Page 123
This selection from Matthew's gospel is taken from the *Good News Bible*, revised edition.

Page 125
Jalâl al-Din Rumi (1207-1273) was a mystic and a poet. This poem is from Franklin D. Lewis, *Rumi: Past and Present, East and West, The Life, Teaching and Poetry of Jalâl al-Din Rumi* (Oxford: Oneworld, 2000), 416. Used with permission.

Page 127
Bahá'u'llah (1817–1892) was founder of the Bahá'i Faith. His given name was Mírza Husayn 'Alí, but he identified himself as Bahá'u'l-lah, which means "Glory of God." This passage is an excerpt from Meditation LVIII, "Praise be to Thee, to Whom the tongues of all . . . ," *Prayers and Meditations of Baha'u'llah*. Copyright Bahá'i International Community.

Page 129
The Hail Mary is a popular prayer among Roman Catholics; it is the essential element of the rosary, a prayer method practiced primarily by Catholics calling for the intercession of Mary, the mother of Jesus. The first sentence is the greeting of the Archangel Gabriel to Mary (Lk 1:28). The second sentence is the greeting to Mary by her cousin, Elizabeth (Lk 1:42). It is also a reinforcement of basic Christian belief in the real divinity and real humanity of Jesus. The closing two lines came into general use in the sixteenth century.

Page 131
Fr. Daniel Berrigan, SJ, (1921–) is a poet, peace activist, and Jesuit priest. The passage is from Daniel Berrigan, SJ, *America is Hard to Find* (New York: Doubleday, 1972), 37. Fr. Berrigan's contribution to this volume can be found on page 27.

Page 136
This selection from the Qur'an is from Surah Al-Hujurat (The Inner Apartments), Dr. Thomas F. Cleary, *The Qur'an: A New Translation* (Starlatch Press, 2004), 256.

Page 138
Padoh Mahn Sha Lah Phan (1943–2008) was Zoya Phan's father and secretary general of the Karen National Union, the largest insurgent group in Burma. This poem is quoted in Zoya Phan, *Little Daughter: A Memoir of Survival in Burma* (London: Simon & Schuster, 2009), 320. Copyright © Zoya Phan, 2009. Reprinted by permission of Penguin Group (Canada), a Division of Pearson Canada Inc and Simon & Schuster UK Ltd. The poem, entitled "To Beloved Daughter Against the Current" originally appeared in UNDAUNTED: My Struggle for Freedom and Survival in Burma by

Zoya Phan with Damien Lewis. Copyright © 2009 by Zoya Phan and Damien Lewis. Reprinted with permission of the US publisher Free Press, a Division of Simon & Schuster, Inc. All rights reserved.

Page 140
The *Book of Common Prayer* is the Anglican service book of the Church of England. Since its introduction in the sixteenth century, it has had an enormous influence on English writings. It has gone through many revisions, both in England and in the other countries of the Anglican Communion.

Page 143
Julian of Norwich (1342–c. 1420) was a celebrated English mystic. This quotation is from *Showings,* The Sixty Eighth Chapter, trans. Edmund Colledge & James Walsh (New York: Paulist Press: 1978), 315. Copyright © 1978 by The Missionary Society of St. Paul the Apostle in the State of New York, Paulist Press, Inc., Mahwah, NJ. Reprinted by permission of Paulist Press, Inc., www.paulistpress.com

Page 145
Augustine (354–430 CE) was born in North Africa to a pagan father and a devout Christian mother. When he was thirty-two he had a profound conversion to Christianity and was ordained a priest and later became bishop of Hippo in North Africa. He was a pioneer of monasticism, a prolific writer, and an influential theologian. *Confessions,* Augustine's most famous work, invites the reader to share his dialogue with God as the author acknowledges the dilemma of his own sinfulness and the way in which Providence has constantly beckoned him to enter into a graced friendship with the Divine. The prayer quoted here is from the *Confessions* Book Ten, Chapter 27, 38.

Page 146
These prophetic traditions (hadiths) were collected by the Persian Muslim scholar Muhammad Ibn Ismail al-Bukhari (810–870 CE) after having been transmitted orally for generations.

Page 148
Julian of Norwich (1342–c. 1420) was a celebrated English mystic. This quotation, "Love Was His Meaning," is from *Enfolded in Love—*

Daily Readings with Julian of Norwich, ed. Robert Llewellyn (London: Darton Longman & Todd, 1980), 67. Copyright 1980 by Darton Longman & Todd Ltd., London, and used by permission of the publishers.

Pages 150–151
Shantideva was an eighth-century Indian master and scholar. His famous work, the *Bodhicharyavatara*, is regarded as the quintessential Buddhist text on compassion, and has been a constant source of inspiration for the great masters of Tibet. The prayer quoted here is an excerpt from *Bodhicharyavatara* Chapter X, Dedication. The second prayer quoted here is often attributed to Saint Francis of Assisi (1181–1226), one of the most celebrated and best-loved saints, who is remembered for his gentleness and, because of his willingness to see God's presence in all aspects of nature, is considered the patron saint of ecology. Research shows that this prayer, which is often published on a card with a picture of Saint Francis, was actually written in 1912 in France by a priest and widely circulated during World War I.

Page 152
Rosa Victoria Calderón de Billig (1886–1964) was the grandmother of Patricia Roberts.

Page 154
This prayer by Richard Rohr, OFM, entitled "Eternal Now Prayer," is used with permission.

Page 156
Rabbi Nachman ben Feiga of Breslov (1773–1810) was a Jewish sage and mystic.

Page 158
Jalâl al-Din Rumi (1207–1273) was a mystic and a poet. These poems are from *The Essential Rumi*, translated by Coleman Barks (HarperOne, 1995) 36, 281. © Coleman Barks, *The Essential Rumi*.

Page 160
Swami Satyananda Saraswati (1923–2009) was a yogi master and guru in India and the West. This excerpt is from his book, *High on*

Waves (Munger, Bihar: Yoga Publications Trust, 2009). Copyright © Bihar School of Yoga 2009.

Page 162
These words to Pete Seeger's song, "Old Hundred," are from *Where Have All the Flowers Gone* (Bethlehem, PA: A SingOut Publication, 2009), 194. Copyright © Figs. D Music (BMI) / Sanga Music Inc. (BMI). Under license from The Bicycle Music Company. All rights reserved. Used by permission.

Page 165
Sant Darshan Singh Ji Maharaj (1921–1989) was a leading mystic and poet. The verses quoted here can be found in Sant Rajinder Singh Ji Maharaj's book *Inner and Outer Peace through Meditation* (Illinois: Radiance Publishers, 2007), 50. Used with permission.

Page 167
Sri Guru Granth Sahib is the holy scripture of the Sikh faith. The holy texts span 1,430 pages and contain the actual words spoken by the Sikh Gurus as well as writings of people from other faiths, including Hinduism and Islam. The selections presented here were translated by Bhai Sahib Bhai (Dr.) Mohinder Singh.

Page 169
This chant is from the *Brihadaranyaka Upanishad,* part 1, chapter 3, verse 28. The *Brihadaranyaka Upanishad* is one of the older Upanishads or Hindu mystic teachings, thought to have developed around 1000–600 BCE.

Page 170
John S. Spong, *Christpower,* arranged by Lucy Negus Boswell (Hale Publishing, Richmond, VA, 1974). Used with permission.

Page 172
Burnum Burnum (1936–1997) was an Aboriginal activist and author. The "Fire Blessing" is printed here with the permission of Marelle and Umbarra Burnum Burnum via Helen Summers.

Page 175
"Prayer for the New Moon" in *Forms of Prayer* (London: Movement

for Reform Judaism, 2008), 250. The Movement for Reform Judaism, The Sternberg Centre for Judaism, London, N3 2SY, England.

Page 177
These words of Elsa Tamez were translated by Gloria Kinsler.

Page 179
Yangbi Lopen was a senior Buddhist monk who addressed the Royal Bhutan Army before the 2003 Low Intensity Conflict. Quotation from Tim Fischer and Tshering Tashi, *Bold Bhutan Beckons* (Copy-Right Publishing, 2009), chap. Hotel Mike and His Warriors—The 2003 Conflict.

Page 180
"Victory is Ours," in *An African Prayer Book* (Doubleday/Random House, 1995), 80. Copyright ©1995 by Desmond Tutu. All rights reserved. Used by permission.

Page 181
Isaac Watts (1674–1748) was an English hymn-writer and theologian. This hymn, originally titled *Man Frail, and God Eternal* was written as a paraphrase of Psalm 90, and is often sung on great public occasions. The words quoted here are from *Psalms of David, Imitated in the Language of the New Testament and Applied to the State of Christian Worship,* (1719), 180.

Page 184
These words are excerpted from Miriam-Rose Ungunmerr-Baumann's *Dadirri*. Used with permission.

Page 188
This selection from the Qur'an is from Surah Al-Baqarah (The Cow), translated by Amina Wadud.

Page 191
Alojzy Feliński (1770–1820) was a Polish writer and politician. The original hymn, *Boże, coś Polskę* (God save Poland), was written by Feliński in 1816 in the spirit of England's *God Save the King*. The hymn's history is complex, with at least three authors participating at different points in time in its creation. Feliński's hymn has undergone

numerous transformations in its poetic paraphrasings depending on the changing political situations and priorities of Poland.

Page 193
Sam Keen (1931–) is a freelance thinker, author, philosopher of religion and a trapeze flyer. This excerpt is from his book, *Apology for Wonder* (New York: Harper and Row Publishers, 1969), 15, 211. Used with permission.

Page 199
Johann Franck, (1618–77) was a German poet, hymn writer and lawyer. This excerpt from his "Schmücke dich o liebe Seele" in *Gesangbuch,* J. Crüger and C. Runge, 1653, was translated by Catherine Winkworth as "Deck Thyself, My Soul, with Gladness" and can be found in *Chorale Book for England,* 1863.

Page 202
The first line of *The Shema Koleinu* is from the *Amidah,* the daily Jewish prayer; the subsequent verses are from Lamentations 5:21, Psalm 51:11 and Psalm 71:9. Their use in the liturgy of the Day of Atonement dates back to ancient times.

Page 204
Dr. Ernest Holmes (1987–1960) was founder of the Religious Science Movement and the United Centers for Spiritual Living.

Page 206
This poem is from Xinran's *Message from an Unknown Chinese Mother: Stories of Loss and Love* (London: Chatto & Windus, 2010), 179, translated from Chinese by Nicky Harman. Reprinted with the permission of Scribner, a Division of Simon & Schuster, Inc., from *Message from an Unknown Chinese Mother: Stories of Loss and Love* by Xinran. Copyright © 2011 by The Good Woman of China Limited. All rights reserved.

Page 208
Poetic interpretation from http://wahiduddin.net/words/bismillah.htm. Used with permission.